Chicago Public Library
C
P
L
REFERENCE
Form 178 rev. 1-94

D1058683

# Small and Medium-Sized Enterprises in the Global Economy

# Small and Medium-Sized Enterprises in the Global Economy

*Edited by Zoltan J. Acs and Bernard Yeung*

Ann Arbor

THE UNIVERSITY OF MICHIGAN PRESS

Published in the United States of America by
The University of Michigan Press
Manufactured in the United States of America
♾ Printed on acid-free paper

2002 2001 2000 1999 4 3 2 1



*A CIP catalog record for this book is available from the British Library.*

Library of Congress Cataloging-in-Publication Data

Small and medium-sized enterprises in the global economy / edited
by Zoltan J. Acs and Bernard Yeung.
p. cm.
Papers presented at a conference sponsored by the Center for
International Business Education and Research, held at the
University of Maryland, Oct. 20, 1995.
Includes bibliographical references and index.
ISBN 0-472-11001-2 (acid-free paper)
1. Small business—Congresses. 2. International
trade—Congresses. 3. Technology transfer—Economic
aspects—Congresses. I. Acs, Zoltan J. II. Yeung, Bernard, 1953–
HD2341 .S5678 1999
338.6′42—dc21 98-40235
CIP

*Grateful acknowledgment is made to the contributors, Zachary Rolnick, and Small Business Economics for permission to reprint the following previously published materials.*
"New and Small Firms in Expanding Markets," *Small Business Economics* 9 (1997): 79–84; "The Internalization of Small and Medium-Sized Enterprises: A Policy Perspective" in *Small Business Economics* 9 (1997): 7–20; "Alliance Strategies of Small Firms," *Small Business Economics* 9 (1997): 33–44; "Small Firms as International Players," *Small Business Economics* 9 (1997): 45–51; "The Exploration of Technological Diversity and the Geographic Localization in Innovation" in *Small Business Economics* 9 (1997): 21–31; "The Production, Transfer and Spillover of Technology: Comparing Large and Small Multinationals as Technology Producers," *Small Business Economics* 9 (1997): 53–66; and "International Technology Transfer by Small and Medium-Sized Enterprises" in *Small Business Economics* 9 (1997): 67–78.

# Contents

## **Part 4.** Technology Transfer in the Global Economy

# Preface

The idea for this volume was stimulated by a lecture on Alliance Capitalism that John Dunning gave at the University of Maryland. While it is well known that the international presence of large enterprises has grown, very little is known about the presence, or the process, by which small and medium-sized enterprises (SMEs) participate in the global economy. In order to better understand this process the Center for International Business Education and Research (CIBER) at the University of Maryland organized a conference of experts on "Small and Medium-Sized Enterprises in the Global Economy," held on October 20, 1995. The conference was organized by Zoltan J. Acs, then Associate Director of CIBER. The primary focus of the conference was on the role that technology and network organizations play in the global activities of SMEs. Participants in this conference examined the role of SMEs in the identification of technological opportunity, technological diversity and geographical localization, technology transfer, R&D spillovers, strategic alliances, and the international diffusion of innovations. The essays appearing in this volume are revised versions of those presented on that occasion.

The primary contributors are, of course, the separate authors. The first acknowledgment should be directed toward these authors who, along with the original publisher of some of the essays, Kluwer Academic Publishers, have granted permission for reprinting in this volume. John Dunning's essay is a revised version of a 1994 paper, with the introduction and conclusion written specifically for this book. We would like to thank Lee Preston for his support, and Ellen McCarthy of the University of Michigan Press for help in expediting this process.

# Introduction

## Small and Medium-Sized Enterprises, Technology, and Globalization

*Zoltan J. Acs*

There is little question that economic activity of all types is moving in the direction of globalization. As we approach the twenty-first century, a worldwide system of production and distribution is evolving, in much the same way as national markets evolved from local and regional networks during the nineteenth century (Chandler 1990). In nearly every economically active country of the world, the importance of international trade and foreign direct investment (FDI) has risen significantly over the last decade.[1] The growth of FDI has been particularly dramatic, increasing more rapidly than either world production or world trade. As a result, both inbound and outbound FDI stocks have increased relative to total investment and gross domestic product in nearly every country (Dunning 1995).

*Globalization* refers to the web of linkages and interconnections between states, societies, and organizations that make up the present world economic system. Globalization creates new structures and new relationships, with the result that business decisions and actions in one part of the world have significant consequences in other places. The growth of global markets stimulates competition and forces governments to adopt market-oriented policies, both domestically and internationally. Modern technologies have greatly reduced the costs of information and of the capabilities to participate in the global economy (Dunning 1993). Countries must join the club. Policies that aim to exclude global participation via trade and investment barriers can be easily circumvented, and they keep no hostages but deprive the countries of global prosperity.

Underlying and reinforcing these globalization trends is the rapidly changing technological environment, particularly in biotechnology, information processing, and telecommunications. Changes in telecommunications and data processing capabilities make it possible to coordinate research, marketing, and production operation around the world. Almost instantaneous communications makes it possible to trade financial instruments twenty-four hours a day, and thus location of resources within firms, industries, and countries is more return-sensitive. Contemporary technical advances are demanding a much closer synthesis and more integrative learning between innovative and production activities. The pressures of global competition force producers to continually innovate and to upgrade the quality of existing products. Yet, at the same time, many firms can no longer acquire or afford all the technological and human resources that they need. Increasingly, they form interdependent and flexible relationships with other firms—including suppliers and competing firms—to fully capitalize on their core competencies (Gomes-Casseres 1996). Interdependence calls for a capacity on the part of firms, individuals, and governments to interact with speed, flexibility, and creativity to the actions of other agents (de la Mothe and Paquet 1996).

In this new environment knowledge and intellectual labor are being mobilized on a more collaborative basis. Firms must develop human resource strategies based on synthesis with educational institutions. They must locate design and production facilities in metropolitan areas that allow partnerships with suppliers and educational institutions, and in places served by governments committed to business-friendly policies. The main form of economic organization in intermediary product markets is increasingly a network of interfirm cooperative arrangements, rather than the large hierarchical firm (Reich 1992).

Before 1980 most FDI was of the "stand alone" variety. Each multinational enterprise (MNE) would exploit its own home-based competitive advantages and coordinate related intrafirm activities across national boundaries through internal mechanisms (Hymer 1976). More recently, however, MNEs are expanding their territorial and functional horizons by acquiring, or gaining access to, new resources and capabilities. The critical feature of strategic asset—seeking FDI, as opposed to market-seeking FDI, is that participating firms recognize that their stand-alone resources and capabilities are *insufficient* to sustain their international competitiveness, and that they need to draw upon resources and capabilities of others to achieve this goal. While there are many reasons why firms form alliances with other firms, the great majority of those concluded over the past decade have been to gain access to new product or process, technologies, and organizational competencies, especially those perceived necessary to advance their core competencies.

Globalization challenges management and students of business economics. According to conventional wisdom, most transnational business activities, particularly those involving FDI or cross-border alliances, are traditionally carried out by large firms. In addition, some people have believed that technological change requires total operations of increasingly large scale,

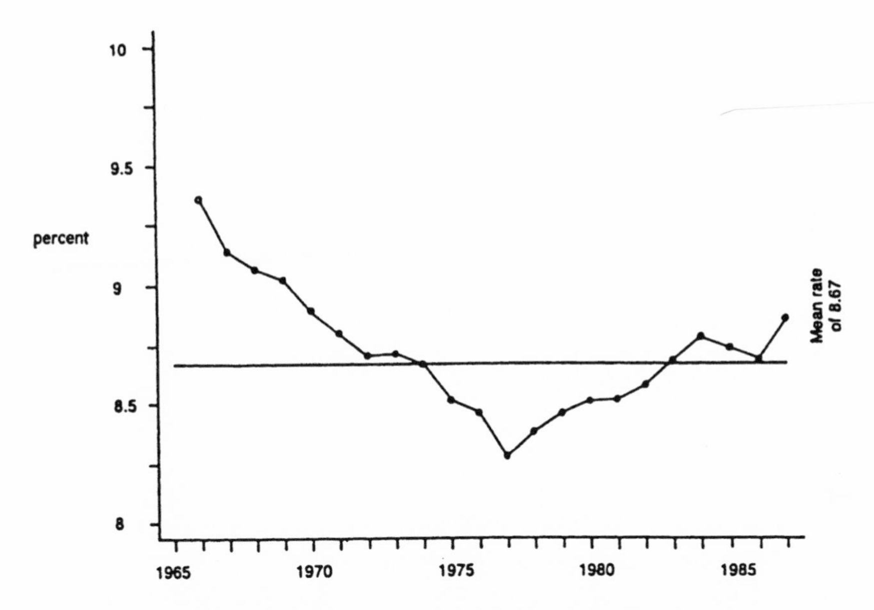


**Fig. 1. Self-employment rate in the OECD countries. (Reprinted from Acs and Evans 1994.)**

along with increasing size of research and development resources. *These views would lead one to expect that small enterprises would decline in importance as they become overwhelmed by global firms exploiting economies of scale.*

There is considerable evidence that these commonly held views are no longer correct. Depending upon the measure of business size examined, the long-term trend toward increasing firm size either decelerated, ceased, or reversed itself sometime between the late 1960s and the late 1970s. An important aspect of the shift toward smaller firms is the self-employment rate. The long-run trend toward less self-employment was reversed in the early 1970s in the majority of Organization for Economic Cooperation and Development countries (OECD). Figure 1 shows the total self-employment rate for 17 OECD countries between 1966 and 1987. The figure shows that the self-employment rate for the 17 OECD countries decreased from 9.4 percent in 1966 (the peak for the period) to 8.3 percent (the trough for the period) and then increased to 8.9 percent in 1987 (Acs and Evans 1994).

Is the apparent resurgence of smaller firms due to the emergence of a dynamic, vital innovative entrepreneurial sector, or is it due to the inability of large incumbent MNEs to prevail in a technologically dynamic global environment (Acs 1996)? Harrison (1994) has argued that the role of SMEs has been overestimated, and that MNEs have been able to prosper in the new global environment by combining four basic building blocks: returning to their core competencies; using new information technologies; forming strategic alliances; and eliciting more active collaboration from their workers. However, this view overlooks the synergy between large and small firms, the strong attachment of small firms to their local economies, the role of small firms in technological change, and the role they play in the growth and evolution of industries (Acs 1995).[2]

In fact, there is ample evidence that small and medium-sized enterprises (SMEs) have not only flourished in domestic economies, but that their international presence has grown as well (UNCTAD 1993, 1998; Oviatt and McDougall 1995, 1998; McDougall 1989; Fujita 1995a, 1995b; Admiraal 1996; and Buckley, Campos, and Mirza 1997). Firms are considered SMEs if they have less than 500 employees in the United States and less than 300 in the European Union. However, very little is known about the processes by which SMEs participate in the global economy. The purpose of this volume is to increase our theoretical understanding of the processes by which SMEs participate in the global economy.

An overview of SME participation in the global economy reveals at least three lines of activity: trade, technology, and investment. The most commonly discussed topic in SMEs international literature is their role as exporters from their domestic jurisdictions to foreign customers. The opportunities and challenges facing SMEs in this role are well known. We do not address these topics in any detail. Instead, we see export activity as linked to other activities that are given greater emphasis here.

The second most prominent issue in the literature is SMEs and technology, and particularly SME supplier connections with larger MNEs in local markets. In their simplest form, these connections involve "intranational exports," that is, domestic sales to foreign firms that happen to be operating within the home country of the supplier. The importance of these connections is stressed by Porter (1993) in his discussion of the role of "related and supporting industries" and Dunning (1993) under the heading of "linkages and spillover effects" of MNEs.

The final issue is the SME role in investment, that is, the connection between SMEs and FDI. SMEs may evolve as multinationals either through their own investments or as a result of the formation of alliances. The essays in this volume carefully examine the questions of why SMEs go abroad, how they do it, and what the consequences of this activity are (Dana, Etemad, and Wright 1998).

In part 1 we start by examining the role of SMEs and the global economy. First, Reynolds revisits an old question: "Do larger markets favor larger firms?" A number of recent analyses and events suggest that the types of large markets currently in development not only provide substantial opportunities for SMEs, but that a dynamic *new* and *small firm* sector is critical for economic growth in these markets. Rather than weak and vulnerable entities that may require subsidies, new and small firms may not only thrive in new global markets, but may be a necessary component for enhanced economic well-being (Lucas 1988).

The reasons why this may be true are examined in the essay by Dunning. He suggests that the global economy of the last twenty years is the epitome of a succession of radical technological and political changes that have created an increasingly porous and complex set of relationships. The single-activity, autonomous firm is now the exception rather than the rule. The net result of the growth of both inter- and intrafirm activities is that the boundaries of the firm have become more porous. Most contemporary firms are multiactivity and are often part of a web of interfirm cooperative alliances. This has shifted the emphasis from a traditional neoclassical theory of the firm focusing on its role as a production unit to one where it is a transacting and coordinating unit. It is this change in the character of firms in general that gives rise to an interdependent role for small and medium-sized firms in the global economy. The essay identifies the extent and character of the changes that have taken place in the dimensions of the three main organizational forms that can be identified with a capitalist economy, particularly those that arise from the globalization of business activity.

Part 2 reviews the role of SMEs as innovators and examines their role in FDI. We start by examining the technological basis of SMEs. Though in the aggregate SMEs spend less on R&D than large firms, they produce almost twice as many innovations on a per employee basis (Acs and Audretsch 1990). In 1993 in the United States, SMEs received 3.8 percent of federal R&D dollars and performed 14.5 percent of company-funded industrial R&D (U.S. National Science Foundation 1996). In 1991 SMEs received 40 percent of all domestic utility patents granted in the United States (U.S. Patent and Trademark Office 1996). This raises two important questions: (1) Why are SMEs superior innovators in the first place? and (2) How do we explain the superior innovative performance of SMEs if they spend less on R&D than large firms?

Why SMEs are superior innovators is examined in the essay by Acs, Morck, Shaver, and Yeung. The critical role of property rights in capitalist economies is becoming increasingly evident. Societies must protect innovators' property rights to the gains from their innovations. An additional angle in the essay is that it also emphasizes an innovator's property rights within an organization. An innovator in a large company only has very limited property rights protection. The new product or process generally belongs to the firm, not the employee who invented it. This reduces creative employees' incentives to innovate for the company. The lack of clear property rights in large corporations creates perverse incentives for both employees and managers. Both can benefit from "free riding" on other people's innovative efforts and results (Zider 1998).

In contrast to innovative employees in large firms, innovators in small firms have three clear advantages: (1) independent innovators can hold clear property rights, (2) they can have every incentive to undertake radical innovations, and (3) they can be largely free of red tape. Thus they argue that SMEs are better at creating radical innovations because they better protect the innovator's property rights.

Acs and his colleagues further argue that the international diffusion of SMEs' innovations is important for global economic welfare. However, SMEs have only limited operations abroad. One reason for this is the presence of barriers to entry. Barriers to entry that limit international expansion are systematically higher for SMEs than for larger firms. Another reason is that SMEs have fewer resources to protect their property rights. The authors suggest that using existing MNEs as international conduits for SMEs' innovations can frequently circumvent resource constraints faced by SMEs in international markets. MNEs can thus serve as catalysts and facilitators of smaller firms' international expansion.

While direct expansion by SMEs is the subject of much discussion, the intermediated possibility had not been given much attention. However, such intermediated modes of expansion are adversely affected by transaction difficulties and intermediators' rent extraction. Acs and his colleagues raise several conceptual considerations important in comparing the two modes of international expansion and identify the conditions for private market arrangements to be efficient.

The next two essays offer examples of the intermediated form of international expansion and the direct mode of international expansion by SMEs. If small firms face higher barriers to entry in international operations than large firms, and they have a more difficult time protecting their property rights, how can small firms become international players? When SMEs invest abroad they generally seek help. In his essay, Gomes-Casseres examines the use of strategic alliances by SMEs (Beamish 1998). He asks three questions: (1) When do small firms use alliances to do business abroad? (2) How do small businesses use alliances? and (3) What effect do alliances have on firms' competitive performance? The essay defines a new unit of competition called a *constellation.* A constellation is a set of firms linked together by alliances. The essay finds that small firms can follow one of two different approaches to alliances, depending on their relative size. Firms that are small relative to competitors and to the requirements of the market tend to use alliances to reach scale and scope economies. Firms that are large relative to the same benchmark rely on internal capabilities to expand. In any event, the evidence shows that SMEs, against the expectations of many traditional scholars, are active players in the international arena.

In the next essay, Kohn examines the direct mode of international expansion by SMEs. He asks the question, "How can SMEs play the international game when they choose not to team up with larger partners?" He finds that most small multinational firms follow a "deep niche strategy": that is, their positions are characterized by market dominance and technological leadership, and by a focus on producer goods. Also, small firms tend to invest in younger industries rather than more mature ones. In fact, Gomes-Casseres and Kohn (1996) found that SMEs had fewer, not more, alliances than one might have expected.

How do we explain the superior innovative performance of SMEs? In part 3 we begin by examining the role of knowledge spillovers. Jaffe et al. (1993) analyzed patent citation data pertaining to domestic university and corporate patents to test the extent of localization of knowledge spillovers. Almeida and Kogut (1995) found that localization of patentable knowledge varies across regions. Semiconductor knowledge in the Silicon Valley and New York triangle tends to be localized. This suggests that the presence of complementary knowledge resources are important for innovation. External resources and institutions appear to be especially beneficial to small firms (Feldman 1996). SMEs benefit from R&D spillovers from university research and private research at large firms (Acs, Audretsch, and Feldman 1994; Anselin, Varga, and Acs 1997; Porter 1998).

But why should this phenomenon of regional networking benefit smaller firms rather than larger ones? One reason, perhaps, is that larger firms, because of their property rights and incentive structure, are more self-reliant and do not emphasize building relationships with other institutions in the region. By definition of a start-up, the personnel in a new company will have a shorter tenure in the company, and more recent experience in other firms (Bernstein 1998).

To study the influence of geographic localization on innovation Almeida and Kogut examine the origins of citations to 170 major patents in the semiconductor industry. Field research, consisting of interviews with semiconductor engineers and other informed individuals, served to complement the patent analysis. They argue (1) that start-ups gain their comparative innovative advantage by exploring new technological spaces that may be overlooked by larger firms and (2) that this process is facilitated by regional networking that permits small firms to obtain and use knowledge more efficiently than large firms. They find that start-ups produce innovations in less crowded technological space than larger firms. That is, *small firms are more likely to explore technologically diverse territories.* Their empirical results pinpoint how smaller firms make radical innovations, and they complement the theoretical conjecture in Acs et al.

While knowledge is localized for both start-ups and other firms, start-ups are more closely tied into regional networks since they depend on networks for critical knowledge inputs. Knowledge was more localized for start-ups than other firms with groups of entrepreneurs playing a crucial role. If knowledge flows are localized, then firms located in distant regions are excluded from knowledge networks. It is this local character of the networks that is their potential link with globalization (Acs, de la Mothe, and Pacquet 1996). Small technology-based firms are attractive acquisition targets for MNEs interested in entering new technological networks. About 10 percent of the 38,000 new high-tech establishments listed in the Corp Tech data base had foreign ownership in 1994 (U.S. National Science Foundation 1996, 6–29).

In the following essay Eden, Levitas, and Martinez survey a large literature dealing with international business, entrepreneurship, and technical change and provide a link between the technological literature on SMEs and the technological literature on MNEs. They examine three aspects of technology: (1) technology as a firm-specific advantage, (2) the costs of technology transfer, and (3) technology spillovers. In each case they outline current views and debates in the field about the role played by the large multinationals that, according to the statistical evidence, are the world's principal technology producers. Finally, they compare the ability of large and small firms to profit from technology. They suggest that SMEs are less likely to be able to properly manage the technology transfer process when problems occur.

In terms of the costs of technology transfer, they suggest that SMEs may face higher transaction costs than large MNEs. Although SMEs, due to their relative size, benefit from reduced bureaucratic costs, they also have fewer resources to devote to search, negotiation, monitoring, and enforcement efforts. They may also be more subject to opportunistic behavior on the part of suppliers and buyers due to their smaller size and corresponding inability to retaliate. Finally, SMEs may be less likely to have a tight appropriability regime protecting their knowledge base, and therefore they may face higher risks of dissipation and its attendant costs. This view is consistent with Cohen and Klepper (1996), who have suggested that while small firms may be superior in the *generation* of new knowledge, larger firms are superior in their ability to *appropriate returns* from these innovations, either by buying property rights, acquiring the firms, or benefiting through spillovers.

If small technology-based firms have in fact become more active international players, then how large a role are they playing in the global economy? In part 4 Buckley examines the role of SMEs in technology transfer, relying for empirical evidence on the United Nations Conference on Trade and Development report on small and medium-sized multinational corporations (UNCTAD 1993). The UNCTAD study on technology transfer found that SMEs, like MNEs, transferred technology internationally from the parent firm. The most common vehicle for international transfer is via a joint venture with a host country company. This however is much less formalized than in large MNEs. Three types of technologies are picked up by SMEs: small-scale technologies, labor-intensive technologies, and specialized high-technology know-how. The latter included biotechnology and microelectronics. These firms frequently utilize joint ventures and non-equity licensing deals and alliances.

The conclusion examines the theoretical and policy implications of the international activities of SMEs. The international diffusion of new innovations is crucial for continuing improvement of global economic welfare. In the diffusion process SMEs face two serious challenges: property rights protection and barriers to entry. If the rate of creative destruction is indeed too low, public policies should aim to increase the creation and international diffusion of innovations by SMEs. The analysis in the essays that follow suggests that policies should aim to reduce the costs in international expansion for SMEs. That is, policies should aim to reduce private market costs incurred for the protection of property rights, to reduce entry barriers, and to reduce transaction costs.

## NOTE

1. For a review of the multinational corporation in the 1980s, see Kindleberger and Audretsch 1983.
2. For a review of the literature on international entrepreneurship, see Dana, Etemad, and Wright 1998.

## REFERENCES

Acs, Zoltan J., ed. 1995. "Symposium on Harrison's 'Lean and Mean': What Are the Questions?" *Small Business Economics* 7 (5): 333–63.

———. 1996. *Small Firms and Economic Growth.* Cheltenham, U.K.: Edward Elgar Publishers.

Acs, Zoltan J., and David B. Audretsch. 1990. *Innovation and Small Firms.* Cambridge: MIT Press.

Acs, Zoltan J., David B. Audretsch, and Maryann Feldman. 1994. "R&D Spillovers and Recipient Firm Size." *Review of Economics and Statistics* 100 (1): 336–40.

Acs, Zoltan J., John de la Mothe, and Gilles Pacquet. 1996. "Local Systems of Innovation: In Search of an Enabling Strategy." In Peter Howitt, ed., *The Implications of Knowledge-Based Growth for Microeconomic Policies,* 339–55. Calgary: The University of Calgary Press, 1996.

Acs, Zoltan J., and David S. Evans. 1994. "The Determinants of Variation in Self Employment Rates Across Counties and Over Time," University of Maryland, CIBER working paper #51, December.

Admiraal, P. H., ed. 1996. *Small Business in the Modern Economy.* Oxford: Blackwell Publishers.

Almeida, Paul, and Bruce Kogut. 1995. "The Geographic Localization of Ideas and the Mobility of Patent Holders." University of Pennsylvania, unpublished paper.

Anselin, Luc, Attila Varga, and Zoltan J. Acs. 1997. "Local Geographic Spillovers Between University Research and High Technology Innovations." *Journal of Urban Economics* 42:7–20.

Beamish, Paul W. 1998. "The Role of Alliances in International Entrepreneurship." Paper presented at the conference on *Globalization and Emerging Business: Strategies for the 21st Century,* McGill University, Montreal Canada, September 26–28, 1998.

Bernstein, Peter L. 1998. "Are Networks Driving the New Economy?" *Harvard Business Review* 76 (November–December): 159–67.

Buckley, Peter J., Jaime Campos, and Hafiz Mirza, eds. 1997. *International Technology Transfer by Small and Medium Sized Enterprises: Country Studies.* New York: St. Martin's Press.

Chandler, Alfred. 1990. *Scale and Scope.* Cambridge: Harvard University Press.

Cohen, Wesley M., and Steven Klepper. 1996. "A Reprise of Size and R&D." *Economic Journal* 106:925–51.

Dana, Leo Paul, Hamid Etemad, and Richard W. Wright. 1998. "The Foundations and Evolution of International Entrepreneurship." Paper presented at the conference on *Globalization and Emerging Business: Strategies for the 21st Century,* McGill University, Montreal, Canada, September 26–28, 1998.

de la Mothe, John, and Gilles Paquet, eds. 1996. *Evolutionary Economics and the New International Political Economy.* London: Pinter.

Dunning, J. H. 1993. *Multinational Enterprises and the Global Economy.* New York: Addison-Wesley.

———. 1995. "The Role of Foreign Direct Investment in a Globalizing Economy." *Banca Nationale Del Lavoero Quarterly Review* 193:125–44.

Feldman, Maryann, ed. 1996. *Small Business Economics,* Special Issue on Geography and Regional Economic Development 8 (2): 71–173.

Fujita, Masataka. 1995a. "Small and Medium-Sized Transnational Corporations: Trends and Patterns of Foreign Direct Investment." *Small Business Economics* 7 (3): 183–204.

———. 1995b. "Small and Medium Sized Transnational Corporations: Salient Features." *Small Business Economics* 7 (4): 251–71.

Gomes-Casseres, Benjamin. 1996. *The Alliance Revolution: The New Shape of Business Rivalry.* Cambridge: Harvard University Press.

Gomes-Casseres, Benjamin, and Tomás O. Kohn. 1996. "Small Firms in International Competition: A Challenge to Traditional Theory?" In Peter J. Buckley et al., eds., *International Technology Transfer by Small and Medium Sized Enterprises: Country Studies.* London: Macmillan.

Harrison, Bennett. 1994. *Lean and Mean.* New York: Basic Books.

Hymer, Steven H. 1976. *The International Operations of National Firms: A Study of Direct Foreign Investment.* Ph.D. diss., Massachusetts Institute of Technology, 1960; and Cambridge: MIT Press, 1976.

Jaffe, Adam, M. Trajtenberg, and R. Henderson. 1993. "Geographic Localization of Knowledge Spillovers as Evidenced by Patent Citations." *Quarterly Journal of Economics* (Aug.): 577–98.

Kindleberger, Charles P., and David B. Audretsch. 1983. *The Multinational Corporation in the 1980s.* Cambridge: MIT Press.

Lucas, Robert E., Jr. 1988. "On the Mechanisms of Economic Growth." *Journal of Monetary Economics* 22:3–42.

McDougall, Patricia P. 1989. "International versus Domestic Entrepreneurship: New Venture Strategic Behavior and Industry Structure." *Journal of Business Venturing* 4:387–99.

Oviatt, Benjamin M., and Patricia P. McDougall. 1995. "Global Start-ups: Entrepreneurs on a Worldwide State." *Academy of Management Executive* 9 (2): 30–44.

———. 1998. "Accelerated Internationalization: Why are New and Small Venture Internationalizing in Greater Numbers and with Increasing Speed?" Paper presented at the conference on Globalization and Emerging Business: Strategies for the 21st Century, McGill University, Montreal, Canada, September 26–28, 1998.

Porter, Michael. 1993. *The Competitive Advantage of Nations.* New York: Free Press.

———. 1998. "Clusters and the New Economics of Competition." *Harvard Business Review* 76 (November–December): 77–92.

Reich, Robert. 1992. *The Work of Nations.* New York: Knopf.

UNCTAD, Program on Transnational. 1993. *Small and Medium Sized Transnational Corporations: Role, Impact and Policy Implications.* New York: United Nations.

———. 1998. *Handbook on Foreign Direct Investment by Small and Medium-Sized Enterprises.* New York: United Nations.

U.S. Department of Commerce. 1996. Patent and Trademark Office. *TAF Profile Report.* Washington, DC.

U.S. National Science Foundation. 1996. *Science and Engineering Indicators.* Washington, DC: Government Printing Office.

Zider, Bob. 1998. "Now Venture Capital Works." *Harvard Business Review* 76 (November–December): 131–40.

PART 1

# The Global Economy

# New and Small Firms in Expanding Markets

*Paul D. Reynolds*

Do larger markets favor larger firms? Will new or small firms have a role in the expanded global economy? If one attends to past experience and the current conceptions of modern economies the answer would be both yes—large markets favor large firms—and no—there will be a limited role for new or small firms in the future global economy. However, a number of very recent analyses and events suggests not only that the types of large markets currently in development provide substantial opportunities for new and small firms, but also that a dynamic new and small firm sector is critical for growth in these markets. Rather than a weak and vulnerable sector that requires subsidies, the new and small firm sector may not only thrive in the new global markets, but be a component that is necessary for enhanced economic well-being.

There is much evidence of the growth of large firms in large markets over the past centuries. The history of industrial economies is the story of the advantages of size-leading sectors to consolidate into oligopolies or monopolies. In some cases this has required, for the common good, government policies to ensure that competition exists. This is usually defined as competition between a few large firms, each with a substantial market share. This may be accompanied by programs and policies that are designed to provide assistance or support for those in the SME sector, to ensure they are not taken advantage of by large, established firms, and, quite often, by actions to satisfy the small-business political constituency.

Such concerns were reflected in the broad range of programs developed within the European Union (EU) in the years preceding 1991, the year full integration of the European market was to have occurred. This large, standardized market was to provide a major advantage for large firms, and there was considerable concern over the viability of the small firm sector. But were the fears for the health of the SME sector justified? Apparently not, for the number of jobs and the amount of economic activity in the SME sector has remained substantial and, in some cases, grown. Analysis of EU country employment, value added, and sales by firm size indicates that SMEs have increased their share on all measures of economic activity up to 1990. In the early 1990s the share of value added and sales may have shifted slightly to favor the larger firms. There was, however, no major shift in employment shares by size (ENSR 1993, 1994, 1995). In fact, many large business organizations—particularly those owned and managed by national governments—have experienced substantial losses.

The same discussions and fears for small business have occurred in the United States and Canada as the North American Free Trade Agreement (NAFTA) has been implemented. While some individual firms may be affected, the impact of NAFTA on the new and small firm sector has yet to be established.

## SMEs in International Trade: A Current Assessment

The fear of large firm dominance in the global market has also been a familiar theme, leading to considerable attention to the current or potential role of new and small firms in international trade. A very recent assessment of SMEs and internationalization has been completed by the Organization for Economic Co-operation and Development (OECD) Working Party on SMEs. Attention was given to eighteen OECD member countries and eight Asian economies (Indonesia, Korea, Malaysia, People's Republic of China, Singapore, Taiwan, Thailand, and Vietnam). Although some new data was assembled in a few countries, the assessment emphasized analysis using existing data, and a number of complications needed to be resolved. For example, most measures of export activity excluded micro firms (0–19 employees). Further, no indirect participation in international trade could be tracked, so the impact of an SME supplying a multinational firm could not be determined (OECD 1995).

The analysis determined that, as of the early 1990s, SMEs had a substantial presence in international trade. About 10 percent of all SMEs (mostly in manufacturing) were involved in direct foreign investment. Within OECD member countries 26 percent of direct exports were provided by SMEs; this figure was 35 percent among the Asian countries. It was estimated that there were about 35,000 transnational corporations in the world, of which 20,000 have less than 500 employees. While only 1 percent of SME manufacturing firms could be considered global, this is 30,000 to 40,000 firms across all OECD countries. A further 10 to 20 percent of manufacturing SMEs have 10 to 40 percent of their sales from exports (to 3 or 4 countries), a total of 300,000 to 600,000 firms across the OECD member countries. Finally, about 40 percent of all SMEs in the OECD member countries are considered to be insulated from globalization in 1995—and 60 percent are not insulated. It is expected that 80 percent of all SMEs will be affected by, or involved in, international trade by 2005.

The analysis concluded that SMEs are currently a significant part of the global market and that their role will increase in future years.

## New and Small Firms and Economic Growth

Analysis of the role of new and small firms in market growth has been hampered by the absence of firm size or firm age indicators in most business registries. As data sets are being revised to provide this information, preliminary evidence regarding the role of new and small firms in economic growth is beginning to develop: cross-national comparisons with European countries, comparisons across different economic sectors within a given national economy, and companions of different labor market areas within a single country. This last is consistent with very powerful examples of prosperous industrial districts.

### Cross-National Comparisons

The development of standardized data on firms, by size, across the EU member states makes it possible to consider the effect of changes in sector activity on subsequent growth in gross national product (GNP). The difference between the total annual sales of small and large firms may be compared through subtraction. If small firm sales growth exceeds large firm sales growth the difference is positive. This was computed for EU countries for three two-year periods and used in a linear model to predict change in GNP for the following periods. The analysis was completed for the EU-12 (predictions to 1991, 1993, and 1994) and for the EU-16 (predictions to 1993 and 1994). Despite the small number of observations the impact is statistically significant. A greater increase in the small firm sales, compared to large firm sales, leads to more growth in the national GNP in the following year (Thurik 1995).

This would suggest that small firms are either a mechanism for transmitting economic growth or an independent source of growth—a source of economic growth not provided by large firms.

### Cross-Sector Comparisons

Another strategy is to compare changes in different economic sectors, using classification of jobs and employment for different types of economic activity. A preliminary analysis comparing 33 to 34 manufacturing sectors was completed for each of seven OECD member countries (Schreyer and Chavoix-Mannato 1995). In this case, the average establishment (not firm) size was utilized in linear models predicting job growth within the same economic sector for the 1985 through 1990 period. Controls for growth in real output and a constant to capture trends in employment were included in the linear models. It was found that average establishment size explained about half the variation in employment growth. Manufacturing subsectors with a lower average establishment size had, even with controls for other factors, a greater level of overall job growth.

Despite the exploratory nature of this cross-sector analysis, it does suggest that the presence of smaller firms is associated with economic sector growth, even when the overall sector, manufacturing, may be in decline. Further, the same patterns were found among all seven OECD member states included in the analysis.

## Cross-Regional Comparisons

An alternative strategy makes use of standardized data sets within a single country. This involves comparing different internal geographic areas, considering SME presence and firm dynamics as related to economic growth in later periods. A program of research on the role of new and small firms in Swedish economic growth has been under way for some years (Davidsson, Lindmark, and Olofsson 1995). Using eighty labor market (or journey-to-work) areas as the unit of analysis, it has explored two aspects of the impact of "simples" (single-site establishments); "branches" (units within a multi-establishment firm); and "tops" (headquarters establishments) on economic change, including (1) the role of regional factors in establishment births and deaths and (2) the role of establishment births and deaths on subsequent economic growth. In Sweden, 99.99 percent of all simples have less than 200 employees and 98.6 percent have fewer than four.

Analysis of the effects of business dynamics on regional economic well-being has indicated that: (1) greater turbulence (firm births, deaths, contractions, and expansions) tends to lead to enhanced economic well-being; (2) there were low correlations among measures of business dynamics (regions tended to be unique in this regard); (3) higher levels of change seemed to have a positive impact even when absolute levels of growth were modest; (4) firms births and deaths tended to have a more positive impact on economic growth than measures of expansions and contractions; and (5) the single most important factor affecting economic growth was simple birthrates.

This is, however, a complicated issue to analyze, and the results are not well established in all OECD member countries. Similar findings were found in an analysis of 382 labor market areas in the United States (Reynolds and Maki 1991; Reynolds 1994). In this analysis, statistically significant impacts of measures of business volatility (firm births and deaths) on economic growth were found. Despite substantial and consistent positive correlations, linear models that controlled for other factors produced small, positive effects mostly related to dynamics in manufacturing. Conflicting results have been found for West Germany (Audretsch and Fritsch 1992). In the U.S. analysis, it appeared that higher firm birthrates may be associated with an absence of economic growth, but regions with higher levels of growth almost always have higher firm birthrates in previous years. Firm births may be a necessary but not sufficient condition for subsequent economic growth.

These analyses suggest that

> neither a high dependence on small firms nor on large firms solely appear to be optimal. The regions which have experienced the most favorable development of economic well-being are those that had a good mix of industries and business sizes, and whose business sector was characterized by a relatively rapid pace of change. (Davidsson et al. 1995)

## Industrial Districts

Another source of evidence of the role of SMEs in producing economic growth has come from local productive systems. Arzeni (1995) points out that with the decline of the mass production model of industrial production, researchers have increasingly come to the conclusion that there is no single best way to organize an industry. The chain of conception, execution, marketing, and commercialization of a specific finished product can be successfully organized by firms in a variety of different ways. One way is through a local productive system (or "industrial district") where there is (1) a dense relationship of business activity in a limited space, (2) a focus on one industrial activity, (3) a production process based on a mass of small firms specializing in different phases of the process, (4) a mix of competitive and cooperative interfirm relationships, and (5) a host community with a local culture that has a mix of supportive sociocultural norms and values and an "industrial atmosphere" (widespread local understanding of the production process along with a diffusion of technical skills and innovation).

One example of substantial regional differences is found in Italy (Pyke 1995), where regions of "new industrialization," like Emilia Romagna, with a heavy concentration of small firms, grew in prosperity, while regions of "old industrialization," like Lombardia and Piedmonte, with a strong presence of large firms, declined. Between 1963 and 1984 Emilia Romagna's real annual income (adjusted for inflation) per inhabitant grew 14 percent, while that in Lombardia and Piedmonte declined 6 and 7 percent, respectively. High levels of out-of-region exports seem to be associated with such growth. Studies of the Italian woolen textiles sector suggested that productivity improvements in the smaller firms offset the higher wages, providing them with lower labor costs. The larger firms do not seem to be able to create these productivity improvements.

While it is not clear what proportion of a national economic activity or growth is provided by these clusters of production excellence, it is clear that some regions are heavily dependent upon these industrial districts. They are very common in Italy and Spain, particularly in the textiles, clothing, or footwear industries. Quasi-industrial districts can also be identified as an important part of more heterogeneous regions, such as the cardiovascular device industry in southern California, art auctioneers in London, optic and imaging industry in the Rochester/Finger Lakes region of New York state, McLaren Vale wine-making in Australia, and the automobile supplier industry in Baden-Württemberg, Germany (Arzeni 1995). These analyses suggest that under some conditions and for certain types of economic production, a vigorous new and small firm sector is not an aberration, but a necessity for a competitive regional economy. Collectively, the SMEs in some industrial districts have created a sustained competitive advantage—for the district.

These four examples suggest, then, that new and small firms may have a major causal role in economic growth. Large firms will always have a major role, but this recent evidence suggests that new and small firms can be an independent source of economic growth.

## Economic Globalization

The changes that are expanding economic markets may be considered of two types: (1) technical advances in communication and transportation and (2) harmonization of the regulatory and institutional context in which economic activity takes place. The first reduces costs and the second reduces the risks associated with market transactions.

The major technical advances have been the reduced costs accompanied by increased reliability and speed in communications and transportation. This has been accompanied by a substantial expansion of English as the language of science, technology, and business as well as the use of ASCII codes to relay electronic information. This has reduced many of the transaction costs associated with delivery of goods or services to customers, or acquiring goods or services from subcontractors or suppliers. Much of this standardization has occurred voluntarily within the businesses' communities seeking more efficiency in their operations.

There has been considerable variation in the institutional structures and arrangements that provide the context in which business operates. A basic objective to be served by regional economic markets—EU, NAFTA, APEC (Asian Pacific Economic Community), MERCOSUR (Argentina, Brazil, Paraguay, and Uruguay)—is to attempt to standardize or harmonize the major features of the institutional and regulatory context. This should enhance the confidence of economic actors that all parties to transactions can be relied upon to fulfill their obligations.

These advances may have different effects on business organizations in different sectors. In some sectors there are economic advantages to consolidation (upsizing). Both technical improvements and institutional harmonization reduce the costs and risks associated with entering into economic agreements with others. At the same time, they improve the control and coordination of multisite firms. This would facilitate economic activity that can achieve advantages through covering a larger geographic and cultural domain, such as found in retail, consumer services, and perhaps the financial and banking services. There has been, in some large markets (such as the United States), a consolidation in retail and consumer service sectors. Internationally, there has been a market consolidation and harmonization in financial services and mass media production.

In other sectors, these shifts can increase the benefits of disaggregation, or downsizing. There is a change in the relative costs and benefits of using internal versus external sources for various goods and services. The advantages of using a formalized, hierarchical structure to reduce transaction costs and opportunism in economic exchanges may be reduced as the technical costs and institutional harmonization reduce the risks of engaging in contractual arrangements with subcontractors, suppliers, and consultants.

Some economic sectors may respond in both ways, consolidating the marketing and distribution of products, disaggregating the production process. The global firms in the automobile industry seem to reflect both tendencies—disaggregation of production, consolidation of distribution and marketing.

## Concluding Observations

Three observations have been discussed. First, there is substantial evidence that new and small firms are major direct participants in international trade and this may grow in the future. Second, vigorous new and small firm sectors may have an independent causal impact on economic growth. Third, the underlying changes that are the source of greater globalization of markets—technical advantages related to communication and transportation, reduced risk from harmonization of regulations and the institutional context for economic activity—may have different impacts on different types of economic activity. Competitive advantage in some sectors may be gained through aggregation (upsizing) or consolidation; competitive advantage may be gained in others through disaggregation (downsizing).

Global markets are likely to be quite varied and turbulent as they expand. There will be many opportunities for new and small firms. Global economic well-being is likely to improve with a vigorous new and small firm sector in international trade. Given these changes, there will be considerable opportunities for individual scholars and research centers—in universities, governments, or private settings—to increase understanding of the mechanisms underlying economic growth and the roles of new and old, small and large firms.

## REFERENCES

Arzeni, Sergio. 1995. "International Seminar on Local Systems of Small Firms and Job Creation: Background Paper." OECD LEED Programme, Territorial Development Service. DT/LEED/WD(95)1.

Audretsch, D. B., and M. Fritsch. 1992. "Market Dynamics and Regional Development in the Federal Republic of Germany." Berlin, Germany: Wissenschaftszentrum Berlin (WZB), Discussion Paper FS IV 92–6.

Davidsson, Per, Leif Lindmark, and Christer Olofsson. 1994. "New Firm Formation and Regional Development in Sweden." *Regional Studies* 28 (4): 395–410.

———. 1995. "Smallness, Newness, and Regional Development in Sweden." OECD Industry Committee Working Party on Small and Medium Enterprises High-Level Workshop on "SMEs: Employment, Innovation and Growth." Washington, DC, June 16–17.

ENSR (European Network for SME Research). 1993. *The European Observatory for SMEs: First Annual Report.* Zoetermeer, The Netherlands: EIM Small Business Research and Consultancy.

———. 1994. *The European Observatory for SMEs: Second Annual Report.* Zoetermeer, The Netherlands: EIM Small Business Research and Consultancy.

———. 1995. *The European Observatory for SMEs: Third Annual Report.* Zoetermeer, The Netherlands: EIM Small Business Research and Consultancy.

OECD (Organization for Economic Cooperation and Development). 1995. "Globalization of Economic Activities and the Development of SMEs: Synthesis Report." Paris, France: DSTI/IND/PME (95) 3. Oct. 16.

Pyke, Frank. 1995. "Comparing Small and Large Firms in Europe: Prospects for Incomes and Working Conditions." OECD Industry Committee Working Party on Small and Medium Enterprises High-Level Workshop on "SMEs: Employment, Innovation and Growth." Washington, DC, June 16–17.

Reynolds, Paul D. 1994. "Autonomous Firm Dynamics and Economic Growth in the United States, 1986–1990." *Regional Studies* 28 (4): 429–42.

Reynolds, Paul D., and Wilbur R. Maki. 1991. *Regional Strategies Affecting Business Growth.* Minneapolis, MN: Department of Sociology. Final Report to the Rural Poverty and Resources Program, Ford Foundation.

Schreyer, Paul, and Michelle Chavoix-Mannato. 1995. "Quantitative Information on SMEs: OECD Approach, Data Collection and Examples of Analysis." OECD Industry Committee Working Party on Small and Medium Enterprises High-Level Workshop on "SMEs: Employment, Innovation and Growth." Washington, DC, June 16–17.

Thurik, Roy. 1995. "Small Firms, Large Firms, and Economic Growth." OECD Industry Committee Working Party on Small and Medium Enterprises High-Level Workshop on "SMEs: Employment, Innovation and Growth." Washington, DC, June 16–17.

# Reconfiguring the Boundaries of International Business Activity

*John H. Dunning*

Once upon a time, there was the firm. The boundaries of its economic jurisdiction were clearly demarcated by its ownership. There were few intrafirm transactions, and all interfirm transactions were conducted between independent parties at arm's-length prices. This is no longer the case. Once upon a time, there were identifiable and autonomous markets, the confines of which were unambiguously delineated by the particular assets, goods, and services being traded, and by the parties to the exchange. This is no longer the case. Once upon a time, there were nation-states, whose political domain largely corresponded with their economic domains, and whose governments produced largely independent macroeconomic and macroorganizational policies.[1] This is no longer the case.

The globalizing economy of the current decade is the outcome of a succession of radical technological and political changes, the lineage of which can be traced back to the industrial revolution of the late eighteenth century. At this former time, the boundaries of firms, markets, and governments were easily recognizable and, for the most part, impermeable. Over the past two centuries, the extent and nature of economic activity has become increasingly specialized, complex, and porous. At the same time, its spatial dimension has widened from the subnational to the national, and then to the regional, international, and global.

Such changes have had widespread implications for both the macro- and microorganization of resource allocation. The single-activity, autonomous firm is now the exception rather than the rule. Most contemporary firms are multiactivity and are often part of a web of interfirm cooperative alliances. Markets are increasingly interdependent, rather than independent of each other; and the consequences of market-related transactions frequently affect institutions and individuals other than those who are the direct participants in the markets. As assets have become increasingly mobile, or "quicksilver" across national boundaries, so the distance between economic and political space has widened; and in the framing of their economic strategies, which affect the competitiveness and profitability of business activities within their jurisdiction, governments need to be increasingly aware of the strategies of the governments of other countries, which offer a comparable portfolio of location-specific assets.

This essay has two main tasks. The first is to identify the extent and character of the changes that have taken place in the character and dimension of each of the three main organizational entities that govern the deployment of resources in a capitalist economy, and particularly those that arise from the globalization of business activity. The second is to look more specifically at the role of government as initiator, overseer, and arbitrator of the economic system that determines the contribution and effectiveness of these entities.

## The Domain of the Firm

At one time, the formal or jurisdictional confines of the firm were assumed to be discrete and coincident with its ownership. Such confines related both to the scope of the value-added activities of the firm, be they process or product based, and to the geographical space in which it operated. Implicit in this assumption was that ownership conferred full sovereignty over decision taking. Without such ownership[2] the firm was presumed to have no legitimacy or authority. All transactions within the firm, whatever their spatial dimensions, were presumed to be the responsibility of the owners of the company—although in practice, this responsibility was devolved to the Board of Directors and executive management. All transactions between firms were assumed to be off-the-shelf and conducted at arm's-length prices. Little acknowledgment was given to cooperative agreements involving a continuing relationship between economic agents or an exchange (or sharing) of resources, experience, information, or advice.

Over the years, the formal boundaries of the firm have steadily receded as a result of the internalization of intermediate product markets and the territorial extension of its activities. The contemporary multinational enterprise (MNE) is both the owner and orchestrator of a complex portfolio of interrelated assets, located in two or more countries. In some instances, these internal markets are closely integrated, and the parent company enjoys advantages of common governance and diversification of risk. In others, the MNE is better regarded as a multi-domestic company in which the foreign subsidiaries operate more or less independently of each other (Porter 1986). Over the last thirty years, and particularly as the range and extent of international production has increased, and as regional integration has facilitated the cross-border specialization of economic activity, an increasing number of MNEs have begun to embrace globally integrated strategies (UNCTAD 1993).

At the same time the range and character of the *informal* boundaries of the firm have also been extended. Like that of intrafirm activities, the recent growth of interfirm agreements has also been in response to the increasing costs of arm's-length transactions; but, unlike internalization, this response is better described as a *voice* rather than *exit* strategy.[3] We shall take this point up further in section 3 of this essay.

The net result of the growth of both inter- and intrafirm activities is that the boundaries of the firm have become more porous. Because of this, traditional analytical concepts are found wanting in a number of respects. First—and this is well known but deserves repeating here—the traditional, that is, neoclassical, theory of the firm focused on its role as a *production* unit rather than a *transacting* and *coordinating* unit. However appropriate this emphasis may have been when firms engaged in one or a few activities and served only limited markets, it is no longer the case today. As several economists (notably Douglass North 1990) have shown, as society becomes more complex, the transaction and coordinating costs of economic activity become more important.[4] This is not only because of the increasing costs of acquiring information to measure the multiple dimensions of what is being exchanged, but also because of those costs associated with enforcing contracts and making credible commitments across time and space, which are necessary to realize the potential of technological and organizational advances.

About a half century ago, there was debate among economists as to the supply side limits of the size of the firm producing in perfectly competitive conditions.[5] At that time, the consensus of opinion was that the constraints to a firm's size were not its rising (marginal) production costs, but were the increasing difficulties faced by managers of coordinating resources, capabilities, and markets, for example, rising transaction and coordinating costs. Although the debate was mainly conducted within the context of equilibrium analysis and firms were assumed to engage in only one activity, it is not difficult to argue that the more diverse the activities of a firm, the higher these latter costs are likely to be, and thus the profit-maximizing level of output will be less.

This analysis suggests that the de facto boundaries of the firm will be limited by its production and organizational competency, and by the size and geographical composition of the market. It follows, then, that any upgrading of the former, or extension of the latter, variables will enable the boundaries of the firm to be pushed out. And, indeed, history is replete with examples of the increased size of firms being brought about by changes in both exogenous variables, for example, larger markets, falling transport costs, lower raw material costs, and endogenous variables, for example, an improvement in labor or managerial productivity; while, from a dynamic perspective, the extent to which the boundaries are pushed out rests on the ability of firms to innovate new, or upgrade the quality of existing, products.

There is, however, another sense in which the boundaries of the firm are being reconfigured. This concerns the extent to which a firm is engaging in informal (that is, nonownership) linkages with other firms that have an impact on their ability to sustain or enlarge their economic activities. Here we may introduce the concept of "soft" boundaries as influencing both the organizational limits and the size and scope of production. Although the de jure boundaries of a firm may require little reconfiguration, as long as it has a 51 percent equity interest in any joint venture it may, nevertheless, be that the minority partner will have something to contribute to the efficiency of the majority partner. This may be no less so in minority-owned ventures, and, indeed, in nonequity alliances, for example, subcontracting, research and development (R&D) agreements, and management contracts. Of course not all such agreements require a recasting of even the soft boundaries of the firm. The key question is the extent to which such agreements, or, indeed, organizational arrangements associated with them,[6] may affect the production and organization activities of firms, for example, by offering advice, providing additional inputs or markets, or by making possible economies in the common governance[7] that in their absence would not have occurred.

There are, of course, a plurality of organizational modes by which the soft boundaries of firms may be widened. These include vertical and horizontal alliances formed to accomplish very specific objectives, such as access to new technology, management skills, learning and organizational capacity, or markets; as well as more general alliances intended to share risks, accelerate the innovatory process, and strengthen the overall competitiveness of the participating firms. These may variously affect a firm's performance. Thus a firm may lower its input prices or improve the quality of its end products by forming appropriate alliances with its suppliers. New markets may be tapped by franchising and other agreements with foreign distributors. A firm may best benefit from technological advances and their speedy application by jointly sharing R&D programs with one or other of its competitors. It may gain the economies of intranational geographical clustering if it allies itself in space with related firms (Porter 1990; Feldman 1994).

Some scholars have argued that the world is entering into a new phase of capitalism, namely, alliance capitalism![8] The name implies that for firms to benefit most from innovation-led production, the upgrading of consumer demand, and the imperatives of globalization, they need to engage in a network of cooperative agreements with other firms. This reflects the fact that economic activity is becoming more interdependent, and in order to exploit their core assets effectively, firms have to combine these with the core assets of other firms—or of public authorities. However, rather than enlarge their hierarchical influence, they prefer to establish cooperative relationships with other firms, namely, extend their soft boundaries. By so doing, they are able to improve and make better use of their own competencies, which, in turn, will help them sustain or push out further their market boundaries.

All these developments, then, point not only to the need for more flexible and readily changeable boundaries of firms, but also to the fact that the very nature of these boundaries should be reevaluated. So while a reduction in the scope of a firm's ownership may decrease its hard boundaries, if such disinternalization is replaced by an increase in interfirm cooperative agreements this may widen its soft boundaries.

It is also quite clear that the nature and porosity of a firm's boundaries are specific to both *industry* and *country,* and sometimes even to a *firm* or *activity.* The porosity of the domain of firms would appear to be most marked in the information and technology intensity, manufacturing, and service sectors (notably in the biotechnology, computer, telecommunications, and financial services industries) and in countries, for example, Japan and Korea, whose industrial culture seems to favor interfirm cooperation as much as intrafirm hierarchies. Moreover, such boundaries tend to be even softer when firms go abroad, particularly where, inter alia, due to ideological and political differences, there are substantial intercountry risks and uncertainties, and where the opportunities for synergistic economies are the most pronounced.

## The Boundaries of Markets

The neoclassical notion of a market is that it is an autonomous organizational entity in which the consequences of the transactions concluded are confined to the participants of the market and are independent of those in other markets, that is, there are no intermarket spillovers or externalities. It is also an implicit assumption of neoclassical economics that the costs of establishing and sustaining markets—be they factor or product markets—are minimal. Indeed, no real consideration is given at all to endemic or "natural" market failure—it being presumed that any inability of markets to perform effectively is due to the distorting behavior of one or other of the participants of the market, or to extramarket forces (for example, the intervention of the governments).

However, as North (1990) and others have demonstrated, as societies become more sophisticated, not only are markets likely to be less perfect (in a Pareto optimality sense), but any imperfection is reflected in the increasing transaction and coordination costs of using this organizational mechanism. Such endemic failures have been well addressed in the literature (see, for example, Wolf 1988). In short, they reduce to the presence of uncertainties, economies of scale, and externalities; and to the increasing public good characteristics of intermediate and final products, which contain a high ingredient of *created* (as opposed to "natural") assets.

In this essay, as we are primarily interested in the boundaries rather than the character of markets, we shall be most concerned with those properties that affect these boundaries. Essentially, these reduce to the externalities or spillover effects of market transactions, which lead to the interdependence between transactions and encourage the coordination of them. Such interdependence is of three kinds. First, some products need to be jointly demanded with others if they are to give the purchaser full satisfaction. In this case, the demand for one product is contingent upon the other being available at an acceptable price; in other words, the markets for the two goods are linked. Second, some products need to be jointly supplied if their combined worth (for example, productivity) is to be optimized. This is especially true of intangible assets, for example, different kinds of information. Increasingly, as the demands of both industrial and final consumers become more sophisticated, several interrelated technologies may be needed to produce a given product. Again, the markets for these intermediate products are linked.

Third, there are the extramarket consequences of particular market transactions. The concept of external diseconomies, and the distinction between the private and social costs of producing a product, particularly where viewed in an environmental context, dates back to the time of A. C. Pigou and Alfred Marshall. The notion of the extramarket benefits of activities is perhaps more recent and is currently best captured in those that arise from an increase in the created assets of firms—especially of innovatory capacity and accumulation of human skills and experience. It is, for example, generally accepted that the social returns of R&D expenditure exceed the private returns;[9] which, inter alia, suggests that the private market for R&D cannot perform in a socially optimal fashion. The issue of apportioning the benefits of an investment no less applies to the upgrading of human capital, and to much transportation and communications infrastructure. The problem arises because the firm(s) investing in these activities do not necessarily capture all the benefits from them, or, if they do, the benefits are spread over an unacceptably long period of time.[10]

In some cases, of course, firms may (and do) respond to the kind of market failures just described by internalizing the extramarket benefits. This is most vividly demonstrated in the economies of common governance of interrelated activities. Indeed, much of the rationale for the diversified firm and for international business operations rests on the benefits perceived to arise from the economies of scale and scope. Such gains, it should be noted, arise as much from the reduction of transaction and coordination costs as from production economies. It surely follows, then, that if such costs play a more important role in economic activity, increasing attention should be given to organizational issues!

A later section of the essay will deal with the implications of the reconfiguration of the domain of markets. Here we wish to emphasize that this reconfiguration may take a variety of forms depending on the nature of the markets. In some instances, the reconfiguration may be to strengthen the influence of arm's-length markets. In others, the nature of the market may be affected with arm's-length transactions being replaced by relational transactions between the parties to the exchange, or between these parties and others affected by it. Much will depend on the relative transaction costs of alternative market arrangements, and these will clearly vary over time and space. The fact that there are unique externalities of international business activities—associated inter alia with producing or transacting in countries with different languages, ideologies, institutions, and organizational structures—suggests that the international business scholar needs to consider the impact of globalization on the domain of markets very seriously indeed; for it is in those sectors that are most internationalized that the boundaries of product and factor markets are becoming most porous. Examples include telecommunications, computers, biochemicals, robotics, and financial services.

## Nation-States

In considering the spatial frontiers of MNE activity we shall distinguish between economic and political space.[11] Economic space comprises the geographical area in which production and transactions are undertaken by economic agents whose center of governance, or residence, is within a particular country. Political space refers to the geographical area comprising the jurisdictional responsibility of a particular sovereign legislature. In the case of a national or federal government, this is usually coincident with a single country, although it may extend to its foreign possessions.

While over the past two or more centuries, economic space has continually widened, from the subnational to the national and, then, to the regional and international level, the main unit of political sovereignty has remained the nation-state—even though, as we shall see, in their policies and strategies, national governments are increasingly having to take account of the widening of economic and other space. In a closed economy, political and economic territory are the same and easily identifiable. The boundaries of a nation-state or a country represent the extent of the jurisdiction of authority and the legitimacy of its governing policy, for example, the national and federal government. Once, however, the economic agents of a country engage in international commerce, political and economic sovereignty may no longer be equated. For example, once a country's firms begin trading goods and services, although the political jurisdiction of its government remains the same, its economic sovereignty is reduced to the extent that it is dependent upon foreign buyers and sellers for part of its prosperity. As a country engages in deeper forms of integration, for example, foreign direct investment (FDI), then, not only are the boundaries of its firms and consumers widened, so also are its geographical sources of wealth.[12]

Most scholars (for example, McGrew and Lewis 1992) tend to think of the boundaries of nation-states as being determined by the extent to which they are politically or economically independent or interdependent with respect to each other. The opposite end of the spectrum of autonomy and self-sufficiency is one in which one country is merged with another. In between the two extremes are various stages and kinds of interdependence. The thesis we are suggesting is that the globalization of the world economy is leading to a watershed in, or a radical reshifting of, the *effective* boundary lines of a country, which we may define as the point at which, as a result of its association with other countries, there is no further effect on its *social* domestic production and transaction functions.

If the *extent* of interdependence influences the effective boundaries of nation-states, the *form* of interdependence affects the degree and character of its porosity. Thus, for example, a regional free-trade area impinges on the boundaries in a softer fashion than a customs union; and this, in its turn, impinges even less than a monetary union. The deeper the integration between nations, the more widespread the implications for sovereignty of the participating nations.

The last twenty years have seen a number of trends, each of which is requiring scholars to reappraise the significance of national boundaries. The first is the increasing mobility of firm-specific assets between countries, one consequence of which is that (some) countries are becoming more like regions within a country.[13] This increased mobility has been especially revealed in the rapid growth of both intra- and interfirm cross border alliances, which, in turn, has been aided and abetted by (1) advances in transport and communications technology and (2) the reduction of barriers to the movement of goods, assets, and people brought about by regional integration.

The ability of firms to "vote with their feet" is one thing. The extent to which they are willing to do so is another. Here a different but related aspect of the changing character of national boundaries is manifesting itself. That is that national governments, by their various actions (or nonactions), are increasingly influencing the competitiveness of location-bound resources and capabilities within their jurisdiction, in a way that determines the disposition of mobile resources and capabilities between countries. At one time, as we have seen, such government action was confined to influencing patterns of trade. Today, it extends to influencing the production and transaction costs of domestic resources, and the wealth-creating opportunities of its firms and people. No longer, then, are government (or country-specific) policies independent of each other. Governments, like firms, may, and do, act as oligopolists; and in consequence their spatial horizons are different than they used to be. They are broader in the sense that by their organization policies they may encourage or inhibit the flow of foreign assets to their borders; yet they are narrower in the sense that other governments may affect the competitiveness of their own assets and sometimes cause domestic firms to relocate or restructure their activities outside their home countries.[14]

There is nothing new about the idea that governments may both cooperate and compete with each other, and that the balance of such interaction may be both country- and time-specific.[15] However, with the convergence of economic structure among at least the major industrial nations, and with the widening of economic space, has come a burgeoning of both quasi-public institutions and intragovernmental agencies. In most cases, these have been activity- or issue-specific, but occasionally—especially in the area of macroeconomic policies—they have been more general. The geographical scope of the arrangements has also varied. In some cases it has been bilateral; in others it has been multilateral. Of the supranational arrangements, some (e.g., as agreed in the UN or UNCTAD) have been informal and nonbinding; others (e.g., environmental and standards legislation in the European Union) have been more binding. The point we wish to stress is that alliance capitalism is leading to more *inter*-governmental intervention, and, in an increasing number of cases, this intervention is taking the form of cooperation. But, at the end of the day, governments often compete with each other for the mobile created assets of firms and, as is demonstrated by the policies of member countries of the European Community and/or individual states in the United States, they have considerable leeway to do so.

By promoting the structural integration of nation-states, the globalizing economy is restructuring the effective boundaries of both economic and political space. While some scholars have gone as far as to suggest that this may lead to the demise of nation-states, the majority point to a change in its functions. Thus, while the EU is leading to a reduced role in some of the functions of the governments of the participating nations (cf. those of the states in the United States with those of the federal government), the macro-organizational actions of such national administrations, in influencing the production and transaction costs of economic activity in their midst, are becoming more important.

At the same time, such policies are increasingly being affected by those of other governments, who are seeking to upgrade the competitiveness of their own resources and capabilities. It is in this sense, and for this reason, that the spatial boundaries of nation-states, and indeed the significance of the location-specific advantages of countries, need to be reconfigured.

## The Response of Institutions to the Reconfiguration of Boundaries

The previous sections have hypothesized that the boundaries of the main organizational forms used to allocate resources and capabilities in a capitalist economy are undergoing a radical shift as the global economy moves from a socioinstitutional paradigm of *hierarchical* capitalism to one of *alliance* capitalism. Such a transformation, which is still in its early stages, is causing the relationships between firms, between markets, and between nation-states (or, more particularly, the governing bodies of nation-states) to be changed in such a way that the boundaries are becoming blurred, and cooperation among firms is becoming as much a feature of capitalism as competition between them.

It is also worth mentioning that the boundaries between different organizational forms are also being reconfigured. Thus as nation-states upgrade the issue of competitiveness on their national agendas, and firms (including MNEs) and governments evolve more cooperative and less adversarial relationships,[16] the interaction between governments and markets is also changing. While much government intervention has long been criticized by economists as market-distorting—except where it is designed to inhibit or regulate anticompetitive behavior by one or the other of the participants in the market—it is being increasingly recognized that in an innovation-led globalizing economy, governments may play an important *market facilitating* role. This they may do both by ensuring the supply of the public goods that private firms perceive to be too costly or risky to provide and by assisting the readjustment of markets to technological change, wherever the social net benefits of such assistance are believed to be higher than the private net benefits.[17]

Finally, the interaction between firms and markets is changing. As its name implies, *hierarchical* capitalism emphasizes the importance of large vertically integrated and horizontally diversified firms in the organization of economic activity. But, as we have already indicated, recent years have seen a growth of interfirm cooperative agreements, which, in effect, represent a "voice" reaction of the participants in the intermediate product markets to reduce the imperfections of those markets, rather than an "exit" strategy of replacing the market by administrative fiat.

More generally, we have argued in this essay that the globalizing economy is changing the costs and benefits of alternative modes of organizing economic activity, as well as affecting the systemic role of government as the organizational overlord of such activity. The responses to these changing costs and benefits by the various organizational forms are essentially fivefold. First, if the costs of supplying the product, asset, or factor service in question are increased (or lowered) independently of the organizational mode, then the appropriate response may be to produce or transact less (more), that is, shift the organization supply curve to the left (right). Clearly this response will be highly sector-specific; but as the transaction and coordination costs of economic activity rise, one may assume that a change in these will have a more pronounced effect on the level and structure of such activity than it once did.

The second response is to replace one organizational mechanism with another. Thus, the growth of hierarchies in the late nineteenth century represented a replacement of (that is, exit from) arm's-length markets; while the nationalization of private firms by the postwar socialist governments of the United Kingdom represented a replacement of the private by the public sector. The third response is to seek to reduce the deficiencies of an imperfect organizational mode rather than to replace it. So, rather than exiting from the costs of inefficient governments by deregulating or privatizing markets, a "voice" strategy would try to make the actions of governments more cost-effective. Rather than acquire subcontractors who fail to meet quality standards or adhere to delivery dates, the contracting firms might prefer to reduce such transaction costs by establishing closer and more productive working relations with such contractors. Similarly, governments, by reducing microeconomic uncertainties, removing market-inhibiting practices, and lowering trade barriers (for example, discriminatory purchasing procedures), might help lower the transaction and coordination costs of both hierarchies and arm's-length markets.

The fourth solution is for governments or some other extramarket institutions (for example, groups of firms) to counteract the intrinsic deficiencies of the market by offering inducements to producers and consumers to behave as if a "first best" market existed. Examples include providing tax concessions and subsidies to increase the private benefits of R&D and training to the level of their social benefits; improving information about the export opportunities for small firms; setting up investment guarantee schemes to protect outbound MNEs against political risks; making certain that patent legislation and procedures properly reflect the needs of innovators; assisting the market in its provision of risk capital, especially for projects that are likely to generate social benefits and are long-term in their gestation; and ensuring, directly or indirectly, that the "hassle costs" of doing business—for example, industrial disputes, inadequate transport and communication facilities, and time-consuming bureaucratic controls—are kept to the minimum.

It is not difficult to think of many other examples of endemic market shortcomings, but most reduce to the presence of *X* inefficiency of one kind or another. But there is another aspect of market failure that economists frequently neglect, mainly because they like to assume human beings behave in a consistent and rational manner and are only interested in the pursuit of wealth. Organizational theorists question this assumption and talk about the bounded rationality and opportunistic behavior of producers and consumers, and about the homo psychologicus of cognitive psychology as compared with the homo economicus of economics.

Is it too unrealistic to extend this idea of psychological man to the mentality or culture of wealth-creating activities by countries and corporations? Even the most cursory glance at the ways in which the Arab countries and the Germans conduct their daily business; or the attitudes of the Japanese and Nigerians to interfirm relationship and contractual obligations; or the ethos of work and leisure of the Taiwanese and Greeks; or the perceived responsibilities and duties of workers, business managers, and governments of the Koreans, Chileans, and Russians; or the cross-border operational and organizational strategies of Nissan and Toyota, or Motorola and Texas Instruments, reveals wide differences in the culture or mentality of wealth-creating behavior. The globalizing economy is affording a new importance to concepts such as trust, forbearance, and reciprocity; and to informal, rather than formal, organizational forms in affecting national competitiveness, and hence the disposition of resources and capabilities.

The extent to which the culture of wealth-creating behavior is an intrinsic characteristic of a country or corporation or can be shaped by exposure to other cultures, by decree or economic pressure, or by a reorientation of personal or business values, is debatable. But there can be little doubt that the forces of globalization are compelling firms and governments to review their respective roles in influencing mental attitudes toward wealth-creating activities. Whether we like it or not, the trade-offs between these and other activities, such as leisure pursuits, are changing; and, whether we like it or not, to a large extent they are being set by countries that place the highest value on competitiveness. The grasshopper's attitude toward life is fine as long as the grasshoppers do not aspire to the living standards of the ant. The trouble is that most of us want to retain our life-styles of work and leisure, but also to enjoy all the material benefits of our economically more successful neighbors.

The fifth response, and one that is particularly germane to international business activity, is for supranational organization arrangements to either complement or replace national organizational arrangements. The argument here is that rather than an "exit"[18] or "voice" response to the costs of organizational failure by national institutions, the best solution would be for some agreement to be undertaken at an international level. The establishment of a range of early post–World War II supranational regimes (GATT, World Bank, IMF, etc.) was a recognition that national organizational forms were sometimes inadequate to optimize the international allocation of resources. With the spread of cross-border hierarchies and the globalization of an increasing number of markets, the areas for supranational intervention seem to be expanding.[19] In particular, the current debate over the widening of the terms of reference of the WTO to embrace competition policy, labor standards, and so on, and the growing pressure for a multilateral investment regime, is a recognition of the inability of national organizational modes to provide a first-best solution to minimizing the production and transaction costs of economic activity in a world in which national borders are porous to the movement of resources and capabilities. At the same time, there has so far been little systematic research on the costs and benefits of supranational governance, and we have no clear indication of the conditions under which the fifth response to organizational failure is the optimal one.[20]

## The Systemic Role of Government

A review of the writings of past scholars on the appropriate role of governments in a market-based economy reveals that little attention has been given to the role of government as a creator and overseer of economic organization as opposed to a participator in the system (Dunning 1995b). Apart from the institutional school of economists,[21] most scholars have either assumed that the setting up and management costs of a market-based system of resource allocation is zero minimal or else they have ignored these costs altogether. At the time of Adam Smith, when most products were simple and natural resource-based, the degree of division of labor was limited, and when most markets were subnational, this neglect was perhaps understandable—although it is perhaps worth observing that in the contemporary world economy, the costs of setting up even a rudimentary market system in a poor developing country are far from negligible. In today's structurally integrated world economy, and particularly in the Triad of advanced industrial economies, such an assumption is quite inappropriate, and it is becoming even less so as the components of the market system become more complex and interdependent on each other.

Even accepting the almost intractable problems of identifying both the first-best system (which is likely to be both country- and time-specific) and the static and dynamic costs of supervising that system, it is nonetheless the case that, with the noticeable exceptions of Stiglitz (1989), Wade (1988), and Chang (1994), most mainstream economists, while implicitly acknowledging this role of government,[22] pay only lip service to it. Yet as Amsden, Kochanowicz, and Taylor (1994) vividly demonstrate, the failure of the East European economies to successfully and speedily embrace a market-based capitalism is at least partly due to the gross underestimation by Western economists of the institutionally related costs of setting up the system. Wade (1988) shows that there have been no such illusions among East Asian economists, who from the early postwar period have recognized the critical role of the state to fund most of the setting-up costs of the market system and those associated with its efficient maintenance. The market system is par excellence a public good; and so it is reasonable that governments, on behalf of their constituents who benefit from it, should bear at least some of the costs of it. This, indeed, is the unique and special macroorganizational role of government, and it is the reconfiguration of this role, as much as its role as a participatory organizational entity, that the globalizing economy is currently demanding.

The precise character of the systemic and market-facilitating role of government is still a matter of debate; but, gradually, with the increasing interaction between the particular macroorganizational strategies of national governments (for example, competition, innovation, environmental, and educational policies), it is rising on the agenda of both these governments and supranational regimes. Except in East Asia, the idea that governments may beneficially coordinate (some of) their organizational arrangements in the same way they coordinate (some of) their macroeconomic policies has not yet gained much credence, but this may well be forced on them in the emerging era of *alliance* capitalism.[23]

## Some Concluding Remarks

The aim of this essay has been to argue that the boundaries of the main organizational entities in a capitalist economy are undergoing radical change as market-based capitalism is moving from being *hierarchical* to *alliance* in character; and as production and markets are becoming increasingly globalized. It has described the extent and form of these boundary changes in respect of firms, markets, and governments (acting on behalf of the constituents for which they are responsible).

The essay has four main conclusions. First, not only are the boundaries of each of the organizational forms becoming more porous and interdependent toward each other, but there is a growing complementarity between them. Such interdependence is demanding a reappraisal of the cost effectiveness of the alternative forms.

Second, the globalization of economic activity is requiring a reevaluation of the optimal way in which the three main organizational entities, namely, firms, markets, and governments, respond to changes in the costs of organizing resource allocation.

Third, not only is globalization causing the systemic role of national governments to become more important, but it is compelling them to give more attention to how their policies might be integrated or harmonized with those of other governments, either formally through customs unions or other regional integration schemes, or by participation in supranational regimes and arrangements.

The fourth conclusion is that scholars interested in the determinants and consequences of international business activity need to modify their paradigms and theories to encompass the implications of *alliance* capitalism for the boundaries of economic activity.[24] In particular the concept of the competitive or ownership advantages of firms needs to be widened to take account of the benefits to be derived from interfirm alliances and networking; while that of the locational advantages of countries needs to give more attention to the consequences of the mobility of firm-specific assets and the role of governments in the ways in which such assets may be combined with those that are locationally immobile within their areas of jurisdiction. More generally, scholars need to give more careful attention to the alternative responses to organizational failure; and particularly those directed to trying to overcome, rather than exiting from, those failures.

The consequences of international business activity may also need reexamination as a result of the growing interdependence between firms, markets, and nation-states. The internal transfer of technology by an MNE to its subsidiary, which has few spillover effects and the results of which only affect the recipient country, is one thing; such a transfer between two independent firms, the success of which depends on complementary technologies being available, and the output of which has social as well as private consequences, is quite another. By the same token, the competition for created assets by national governments, may, if it leads to the establishment or strengthening of supranational institutions that may constrain that behavior, affect the cross-border alliance-related strategies of MNEs; while a harmonization of national technical and environmental standards may have no less important consequences for the kinds of value-added activities (as well as their externalities) that MNEs and other firms undertake in particular countries.

It may be this essay has exaggerated the distinctive nature and consequences of alliance capitalism and the reconfiguration of the frontiers of international business activity. Only time will tell whether this is so or not.

## NOTES

1. By macroorganization we mean the organization of a country's resources and capabilities, undertaken by governments on behalf of their constituents; and by microorganization we mean the organization of a firm's or individual's resources and capabilities.
2. Or at least 51 percent of the (voting) equity of share holding.
3. The concept of "voice" and exit strategies was first put forward by Albert Hirschman (1970) to explain the responses of firms or nation-states to threats to their sovereignty or economic prosperity. He postulated two such responses, namely, "exit" to a better alternative, and "voice" which he defined as "any attempt at all to change rather than escape from an objectionable state of affairs (ibid., 30).
4. When the spatially specific transaction costs are added to the North model, then the significance of these costs further increases.
5. See particularly Knight 1921, Sraffa 1926, Kaldor 1934, and Robinson 1934.
6. As, for example, exerted by the banks on the German and Japanese systems of corporate governance (Prowse 1995).
7. Albeit perhaps for a limited time period.
8. As described, for example, in Best 1990, Dunning 1994 and 1995a, Gerlach 1992, and Lazonick 1992. To quote from Dunning 1995a, "the expression *alliance capitalism* should be perceived partly as a socio-cultural phenomenon and partly as a techno-organizational one. The former suggests a change in the ethos and perspective

towards the organization of capitalism, and, in particular, towards the relationships between the participating institutions and individuals. The latter embraces the formal structure of the organization of economic activity, including the management of resource allocation and growth. Alliance capitalism is an eclectic concept. It suggests both cooperation and competition *between* institutions (including public institutions) and between interested parties *within* institutions. *De facto,* it is also leading to a flattening out of the organizational structure of decision-taking of business enterprises, with a pyramidal chain of command being increasingly replaced by a more heterarchical inter-play between the main participants in decision taking" (466).

9. One estimate is that the average social returns to R&D exceed those appropriated by the innovating firms by 50 to 100 percent (Aaron and Schultze 1992).

10. Implicit in these kinds of externalities is the "free rider" issue—which, of course, can work either to the advantage *or* disadvantage of firms, depending on whether they, or their competitors, are enjoying the "free ride."

11. There are, of course, other kinds of space, e.g., cultural and ideological space; but for the purposes of this paper we shall consider these only as they affect economic and political space.

12. This may lead to a divergence between gross national product (GNP) and gross domestic product (GDP). Gross national product is the output produced by the residents of a country including the income earned on foreign assets. It is equal to gross domestic product plus income earned in foreign countries by its own residents (including subsidiaries of its firms) less income accrued to foreign residents on assets they own within their domestic territory. See Dunning (1988), chapter 4.

13. Compare countries in the European Union to states in the United States.

14. For another, but complementary, view on the economic jurisdiction of national governments, see Helm 1989.

15. We appreciate that in classical and neoclassical economics, the concept of competing governments had no place. But in the late-twentieth-century globalizing economy, in which national competitiveness is innovation-driven, where many assets are mobile across national boundaries, and where there is substantial unemployment, this particular tenet of neoclassical economics no longer holds true.

16. Although the form and extent of the cooperation varies markedly between countries. Compare, for example, the various forms of government/firm interaction in East Asian countries with those in the United States.

17. The subject of the optimal "social" investment in dynamic public goods is one that has so far received only scant attention in the literature.

18. Paralleling an "exit" response to rising costs, one could also consider an entry response to rising benefits of a particular organizational form.

19. No less are such institutions proliferating in a variety of noneconomic fields, e.g., the environment, technical standards, defense, health, crime-related issues, etc. See Eden and Hampson 1990.

20. It is hoped that some current research by David Vines (of Oxford University) and David Currie (of the London Business School) will help shed light on these issues. For a brief description of this research, see Currie and Vines 1992.

21. For succinct accounts of the evolution and contemporary views of this school see North 1990 and Dunning 1995.

22. E.g., Friedman 1962; Wolf 1988.

23. For an excellent analysis of recent changes in the macroorganizational policies

published by East Asian and Latin American governments, especially toward innovation, trade, industrial development, and competitiveness, see Bradford 1994a and 1994b.

24. An exploratory attempt to examine the implications of alliance capitalism for the eclectic paradigm of international production has been made by the present author (see Dunning 1995a).

## REFERENCES

Aaron, H. J., and C. L. Schultze. 1992. *Setting Domestic Priorities: What Can Government Do?* Washington, DC: The Brookings Institution.

Amsden, A., J. Kochanowicz, and L. Taylor. 1994. *The Market Meets Its Match: Restructuring the Economies of Eastern Europe.* Cambridge, MA, and London: Harvard University Press

Best, M. 1990. *The New Competition: Institutions of Restructuring.* Cambridge, MA: Harvard University Press.

Bradford, C. I. 1994a. *The New Paradigm of Systemic Competitiveness: Toward More Integrated Policies in Latin America.* Paris: OECD.

———. 1994b. *From Trade-Driven Growth to Growth-Driven Trade: Reappraising the East Asian Development Experience.* Paris: OECD.

Chang, H. J. 1994. *The Political Economy of Industrial Policy.* New York: St. Martin's Press.

Currie, D., and D. Vines. 1992. "A Global Economic Policy Agenda for the 1900s: Is There a Special British Role?" *International Affairs* 68 (4): 585–602.

Dunning, J. H. 1988. *Multinationals, Technology and Competitiveness.* London and Boston: Unwin Hyman.

———. 1994. *Globalization, Economic Restructuring and Development.* Geneva: UNCTAD, The 6th Prebisch Lecture.

———. 1995a. "Reappraising the Eclectic Paradigm in the Age of Alliance Capitalism." *Journal of International Business Studies* 26 (3): 461–92.

———. 1995b. *Governments and the Macro-Organization of Economic Activity: An Historical and Spatial Perspective.* Paper presented to Carnegie Bosch Conference on Governments, Globalization and Competitiveness, Washington, DC, June.

Eden, L., and F. O. Hampson. 1990. *Clubs Are Trumps; Towards a Taxonomy of International Regimes.* Ottawa Center for International Trade and Investment Policies. Carleton University, C/TQS, 90–102.

Feldman, M. P. 1994. *The Geography of Innovation.* Dortrecht: Kluwer Academic Publishers

Friedman, M. 1962. *Capitalism and Freedom.* Chicago and London: University of Chicago Press.

Gerlach, M. L. 1992. *Alliance Capitalism: The Social Organization of Japanese Business.* Oxford: Oxford Press.

Helm, D., ed. 1989. *The Economic Borders of the State.* Oxford: Oxford University Press.

Hirschman, A. 1970. *Exit Voice and Loyalty.* Cambridge, MA: Harvard University Press.

Kaldor, N. 1934. "The Equilibrium of the Firm." *Economic Journal* 44:70–71.

Knight, F. H. 1921. *Risk, Uncertainty and Profit.* Boston and New York: Houghton Mifflin.

Lazonick, W. 1992. "Business Organizational and Competitive Advantage: Capitalism Transformations in the Twentieth Century." In G. Dosi, R. Giannetti, and P. A. Toninelli, eds., *Technology and Enterprise in Historical Perspective.* Oxford: Clarendon Press.

McGrew, A. G., and P. G. Lewis, eds. 1992. *Global Politics: Globalization and the Nation State.* Cambridge: Polity Press.

North, D. 1990. *Institutions, Institutional Change and Economic Performance.* Cambridge: Cambridge University Press.

Porter, M. 1986. *Competition in Global Industries.* Boston: Harvard Business School Press.

Porter, M. E. 1990. *The Competitive Advantage of Nations.* New York: Free Press.

Prowse, S. D. 1995. *Financial Markets, Institutions and Instruments.* Oxford: Basil Blackwell.

Robinson, E. A. G. 1934. "The Problem of Management and the Size of Firms." *Economic Journal* 44:240–54.

Sraffa, P. 1926. "The Laws of Return under Competitive Conditions." *Economic Journal* 36:535–50.

Stiglitz, J. 1989. *The Economic Role of the State.* Oxford: Basil Blackwell.

UNCTAD. 1993. *World Investment Report 1993, Transnational Corporations and Integrated International Production.* New York: UN, Sales No. E.93.II.A.14.

Wade, R. 1988. "The Role of Government in Overcoming Market Failure in Taiwan, Republic of Korea and Japan." In *Achieving Industrialization in East Asia,* ed. H. Hughes. Cambridge: Cambridge University Press.

Wolf, M. 1988. *Markets or Governments.* Cambridge, MA: MIT Press.

PART 2

# Small and Medium-Sized Enterprises, Innovation, and Foreign Direct Investment

# The Internationalization of Small and Medium-Sized Enterprises

*Zoltan J. Acs, Randall Morck,*
*J. Myles Shaver, and*
*Bernard Yeung*

Most of the giant corporations that dominate the landscape of the emerging global economy began as small businesses.[1] In many cases, the rise of these companies was due to their founders developing radical new skills, knowledge, and information. Henry Ford made the automobile an affordable consumer good with his use of assembly line production. William Boeing applied military technology to civilian aircraft production. John D. Rockefeller built a worldwide distribution system. Bill Gates created a standard computer operating system.

In the early decades of the twentieth century, Joseph Schumpeter (1934, 1942) wrote of the process of *creative destruction*, whereby the continual creation of new ideas by innovative firms steadily destroys the positions of stagnant firms. This process, or one much like it, is now thought by many mainstream economists to be fundamental to the prosperity of a capitalist economy. The continued ability of start-up companies to challenge industry leaders is thus of critical public policy concern. There are two key factors in the economic environment that gain importance: property rights and barriers to entry.

The employees of large firms are part of a team. Any innovation belongs to the firm, or at best to the team. This diffusion of *property rights*, along with bureaucratic inertia and other problems characteristic of large firms, dampen potential innovators' incentives to be creative. Thus, we argue that smaller firms are better at creating radical innovations because they better protect the innovator's property rights (National Academy of Engineering 1995).

Small and medium-sized firms, however, have only very limited operations abroad. One reason for this is *barriers to entry*. These can be natural:

financial market imperfections, differences in legal systems, cultures and languages can make international business ventures risky for small and medium-sized firms. Barriers to entry that limit international expansion are systematically higher for smaller firms than for larger firms.

We suggest that these barriers faced by SMEs in international markets can frequently be circumvented by using existing multinationals as international conduits for international expansion. Multinationals can be catalysts and facilitators of smaller firms' international expansion. While the direct mode of expansion by small firms is the subject of much discussion, the intermediated possibility has not been given much attention. We compare the two modes of international expansion, direct and intermediated, and identify the conditions for private market arrangements to be efficient.

In the next section, we outline the importance of small and medium-sized firms for economic growth. In the third section, we discuss small and medium-sized firms' patterns of internationalization and propose some economic explanations. In the fourth section, we discuss the role of intermediated expansion via large multinational firms. Section five contains the policy implications, and the final section summarizes the essay.

## The Importance of Small and Medium-Sized Firms to Economic Growth

Mainstream economists increasingly accept that the fundamental force behind sustained improvement in the standard of living of market economies is *creative destruction*, as described by Schumpeter (1934). In the process of *creative destruction*, the continual emergence of "creative" new ideas underlies the sustained growth of capitalist economies. The ongoing "destruction" of firms that fail to innovate is the less attractive, but essential, aspect of economic growth (Acs and Audretsch 1991; Audretsch 1995).

### Creative Destruction and Smaller Firms

Schumpeter argued that innovations give firms temporary monopolies: until someone else duplicates or betters their innovation, they have no competitors on the same playing field. Since developing, producing, and marketing products based on new ideas is costly, Schumpeter felt these temporary monopolies to be essential; they generate funds to finance further innovation. Because large firms are most able to develop and retain expertise in these areas, and thus reap maximum returns on their temporary monopolies, Schumpeter (1942) saw innovation as increasingly an activity of very large companies. He feared that the increasing bureaucratization of big companies, which was becoming evident even in his time, might eventually choke innovative effort in large firms and lead to macroeconomic stagnation.

In fact, in the modern economy, innovation remains largely the work of smaller firms. In a study of previously stagnant industries, Acs and Audretsch (1988) find the correlation of patents with rate of product and production innovation to be quite low among larger firms, but to be much higher among smaller firms.[2] In short, larger firms are less successful innovators. The same study also finds that industries in which large firms appear more dominant have higher levels of innovative activities, but these innovative activities mostly occur in smaller firms in those industries.[3] That is, smaller firms are the innovators in more innovative industries.[4]

## Property Rights

The critical role of property rights in maintaining the prosperity of capitalist economies is becoming increasingly evident, especially as more information about why economic growth in socialist countries, and the many third world countries that imitated them, was so low.[5] People must be able to keep a reasonable portion of the fruits of their labors or they will not work.

Society must protect innovators' property rights to the gains from their innovations. The creation and application of new knowledge are fundamentally the work of human beings. An innovator in a large company often has only very limited property rights in her innovation. The new product or process generally belongs to the firm, not the employee who invented it. Even in organizations that share profits with their employees, creative employees must share the returns to their innovative effort with many other employees, even when their names are distinctly associated with an innovation.[6] *This reduces creative employees' incentives to work hard for the company.*

The lack of clear property rights in large corporations creates perverse incentives for both employees and managers. Both can benefit from "free riding" on other people's innovative efforts and results. If someone else in the company devises a new product, everyone benefits; so everyone sits back and wishes their colleagues good luck. Furthermore, the job security, bureaucratic promotion process, and incentives to conform that characterize careers in a large company may dull incentives to be truly creative. Employees and managers may turn their creative efforts toward the extraction of resources from the corporation rather than toward socially useful innovation.

The suboptimal incentive structures in many large corporations can allow bureaucratic inertia to drive corporate decisions. Managers' and employees' interests lie in protecting their claims on the firm's cash flows. Thus, when firms try to overcome the "free rider" problem by assigning bonuses only to those employees directly involved in an innovation, this may actually stifle more radical initiatives. This is because senior employees and managers, who were involved in past innovations, may push for refinement to those older ideas (which generate income for them), rather than more radical innovations (which reward only younger innovators). This might take the form of directing corporate resources toward "ideas with proven track records" or "lower risk."

Indeed, if radical new ideas threaten the values of the older innovations, senior people in the firm actually have a monetary incentive to stifle the new ideas! Even where innovations merely require substantial adaptive effort from older employees, pressures to retard change may result. These pressures may manifest themselves as bureaucratic delays, funding problems, or administrative roadblocks. Thus, large corporations may pay inadequate attention to radically new ideas.

These problems may be especially intractable in large publicly held firms, where managers' interests align least with value maximization. Cockburn and Henderson (1995) report privately held pharmaceuticals firms (presumably with managers under greater pressure to maximize profits) to have more linkages with public sector research organizations than publicly held pharmaceuticals firms have. They find such linkages to be strongly associated with innovative success. They also find privately held firms to adopt better innovation development procedures more quickly.

In contrast to innovative employees in large firms, independent innovators can hold clear property rights where the legal and economic systems permit it, can have every incentive to undertake radical innovations, and can be largely free of red tape. Thus, smaller firms serve as better vehicles for innovation.

## Barriers to Entry

Why, then, are large firms so important in modern economies? We believe there are a number of barriers to entry, both natural and deliberate, that frequently prevent new start-up firms from gaining market share. Acs and Audretsch (1988) show that a high concentration ratio has a greater negative impact on small firm innovation than on large firm innovation.[7] If concentration ratio is related to entry barriers, as many economists believe, we can infer that in industries with higher entry barriers, smaller firms become less innovative. We now examine several forms these barriers might take.

*Financing Problems*

Smaller firms must be able to grow quickly to apply innovations to large-scale production. Ready access to capital seems of critical public policy concern here. As Schumpeter recognized, economic growth is dependent on a sophisticated financial system. People with money but no ideas and people with ideas but no money must be brought together. This is what financial markets and institutions do. King and Levine (1993) show that developing countries with more advanced financial systems have faster economic growth, all else equal. This finding is consistent with the view that poor access to capital can stymie the expansion of innovative small firms, to the detriment of the economy as a whole.[8]

It is arguable that large corporations remain important in modern industrial economies because of the formidable resources they can direct at innovation, and the speed with which they can undertake the large-scale exploitation of innovations. These advantages essentially stem from access to capital and perhaps can compensate in many ways for the poor property rights protection large firms offer innovators.

Much of the modern literature in this area stems from Diamond (1985, 1989, 1991) and emphasizes the information collection and processing functions of banks, and the idea of creditors' reputations. According to Diamond banks invest in acquiring information about creditors, while creditors acquire reputations as creditworthy. Because acquiring information and establishing reputations are both costly and subject to various moral hazard and adverse selection problems, small firms have imperfect access to capital.

Venture capitalists step into this information gap to act as intermediaries between large investors who lack information and independent innovators who lack capital. However, they usually demand roles in management decisions and still require insiders to put up substantial funds.[9] Thus, insiders' wealth constrains such firms' growth. Evans and Jovanovic (1989) and Holtz-Eakin et al. (1994a, 1994b) present empirical evidence supporting this view.

This limits the size of the physical operations innovators can establish, and the number of people with administrative, operations, and marketing expertise they can hire. Thus, their imperfect access to capital may force new, innovative firms to begin with very small-scale production. This, in turn, limits the profits their innovations generate. In contrast, large firms can readily use internal capital reserves or raise funds on financial markets.

Thus, a large multinational can begin marketing an innovation around the world almost immediately. This lets larger firms earn higher returns than smaller firms on similar innovations.

*Imperfect Information*

Many barriers to entry are ultimately due to new entrants' information disadvantages or others' poor information about the new entrant.[10] Poor information about labor, raw materials, or output market conditions can lead new entrants to make costly mistakes. New market entrants also may find it difficult to attract good workers and support firms because employment and contracts with established firms, especially larger ones, are seen as less risky.

However, steady entry might erode these informational barriers. Later entrants can learn from the mistakes of early entrants. Also, a higher steady flow of entrants reduces suppliers' and workers' dependence on established firms and thus their resistance to switching jobs and business partners. In other words, more frequent new market entry reduces information-based entry barriers.

*Entry Barriers Erected by Entrenched Firms*

Other entry barriers are erected by established firms resolved to maintain their profits by deterring prospective new competitors. A popular view of such barriers among economists is of established firms colluding to overcharge customers and build up war chests, which they then can use to finance predatory pricing to drive away new competitors.

A sensible antitrust regime can work to limit this sort of behavior, but a complete elimination of market power is neither feasible nor desirable. After all, a critical feature of the process of creative destruction is that innovators should benefit from short-term monopolies due to their innovations.[11]

*Entry Barriers Erected by Government*

Perhaps the highest and most economically damaging entry barriers are those erected by governments. Government regulations and restrictions, legal logistics, taxes, and corruption increase the costs of establishing a new firm. Baumol (1990), Shleifer and Vishny (1993), and Murphy, Shleifer, and Vishny (1993) argue that artificial barriers to entry encourage innovative people to invest in exploiting the system, rather than in socially useful innovation.

Government-organized barriers to entry in developed countries are usually more subtle. Restrictions on entry into "culturally sensitive" industries like broadcasting and magazines are on the books in Canada. Lenway, Morck, and Yeung (1996) present evidence that U.S. government protection keeps inefficient old firms afloat and can reduce innovative firms' payoff and thus interest to enter. In the United States, trade barriers against wood products, agricultural goods, automobiles, and many other imports act as barriers to foreign entrants. In many countries, inspection procedures, safety standards, environmental standards, and other seemingly worthwhile bureaucratic practices may mask barriers to entry that really serve to protect politically entrenched special interests.

The ubiquitous nature of government-created barriers to entry throughout the developed and developing world is undeniable. Larger firms may find government-created entry barriers easier to overcome than do small firms or independent innovators. Large firms have more resources, contact, and clout. They can afford delays, lawyers, bribes, and campaign contributions.

*Property Rights, Entry Barriers, and Innovation*

The elimination of entry barriers and the protection of property rights creates a fertile environment for Schumpeterian innovation (Thurik 1996). Abundant anecdotal evidence suggests that economies with a high proportion of smaller firms are often more dynamic. In Hong Kong, Taiwan, and other parts of Southeast Asia, entry barriers appear to be low, and small and medium-sized firms' entry rates and market shares are both high. These regions' economic growth is well above the global average. The rapid growth of South Korea in the 1980s was accompanied by an increasing market share for small and medium-sized firms, probably a consequence of the elimination of credit rationing policies that favored large firms (Nugent 1996).

China's recent rapid growth is also linked to the emergence of many new small firms in village townships and in coastal areas, often in new industries. The economies of the Eastern bloc under socialism, in contrast, relied on gigantic state-owned enterprises. Even without the perverse incentives of socialism, it is arguable that such gigantic enterprises were incapable of maintaining a pace of innovation to match that set by creative destruction in the West. Recently, after painful efforts to liberalize their economies, some Eastern bloc countries are beginning to grow and simultaneously to depend more heavily on small and medium-sized firms.[12]

In summary, for the global economy the fundamental driving force behind rising living standards is the ability to innovate. Radical innovations are more likely to take place in small firms than large firms because of the advantages that small firms offer in protecting property rights. Refinement and full-fledged commercialization of innovations are more likely to take place in larger firms because of the availability of resources. High rates of innovation therefore require property rights protection and low barriers to entry.

## International Expansion by Small and Medium-Sized Firms

Given that smaller firms are important initiators of innovation, the internationalization of these firms would represent a global diffusion of innovation. In this section, we first describe some empirical observations about the international expansion of smaller firms and then discuss some theoretical explanation for them. Our basic point is that barriers to entry that limit international expansion are systematically higher for smaller firms than for larger firms (Fujita 1995). What follows is evidence that this is so, and explanations for why it is so.

### Smaller Firms Are Homebodies

A way to quantify smaller firms' multinational operations relative to those of larger firms is to ask whether the formers' share of foreign direct investment exceeds their market share in their home economies. The UN report on "Small and Medium-Sized Transnational Corporations" (1993) suggests that, among developed countries with high outward foreign direct investment activities, small and medium-sized firms conduct disproportionately less outward foreign direct investment. For example, small and medium-sized firms in 1982 employed 33.5 percent of U.S. workers in the manufacturing sector. However, small and medium-sized firms accounted for only 1.1 percent of all employment by U.S.-owned foreign affiliates in that sector.

In the United States, small and medium-sized firms accounted for about 98 percent of all business establishments in 1982, but they accounted for only about 20 percent of all multinational firms in 1988. In the United States, roughly 35 percent of large publicly traded firms are multinationals (Morck and Yeung 1991). Assuming this to be the proportion of all large firms that are multinationals, simple arithmetic reveals less than 0.2 percent of small and medium-sized firms to have multinational operations! The same pattern occurs in Italy, Japan, Sweden, and the United Kingdom.[13] Moreover, what little international investment small and medium-sized firms do undertake is a recent phenomenon. According to the UN report, about two-thirds of foreign direct investment by small and medium-sized firms occurred after 1980.[14]

Exporting is an initial step toward international expansion. Small and medium-sized firms' share of exports is also disproportionately lower than their share of home economy sales. However, the disparity here is less dramatic than for foreign direct investment. For example, in Italy, small and medium-sized firms' share of home economy sales is 49 percent, and their share of exports is 45 percent, which is only marginally less. However in Japan, the export share is about 12.9 percent while their share of home economy sales is 61.4 percent.[15]

Finally, international expansions by smaller firms are more likely to fail. Newbould et al. (1978) show slightly better performance from larger firms. Evans et al. (1991) and others confirm this finding. Based on inward foreign direct investment made in the United States in 1987, Shaver, Mitchell, and Yeung (1995) show that the survival probability of foreign subsidiaries in the United States is higher when the parent is publicly traded. Larger firms are more likely to be publicly traded.

## Why Do Smaller Firms Stay at Home?

If, as we have argued, smaller firms can be vehicles for innovation, their strong links to their home economies would seem to be economically sub-optimal. Why are small firms generally homebodies? There are two caveats that must be kept in mind in interpreting the preceding numbers, and then two broad classes of reasons. We first consider the caveats.

### *Caveat (i): Only Some Small Firms Are Innovators*

The most important small and medium-sized firms are those that carry radical innovations; however, these need not be the majority of smaller firms. Many smaller firms undertake no innovative activity. Some may be serving local niche markets relying on the owner's control. Some simply have no competitive advantage to justify international expansion. Others are unable to expand without the owner losing control. Still other small firms might be unsuccessful innovators. The fact that overseas expansion is not a general characteristic of smaller firms does not mean that those smaller firms that would benefit from it are unable to expand abroad.

Indeed, there is some evidence that what foreign direct investment smaller firms undertake does come from firms that look like Schumpeterian innovators. Smaller firms that expand abroad are more profitable than those that do not. The former report profit to sales ratios of 7.9 percent in 1990, while the latter report only 4.2 percent. Smaller multinational firms also invest more in innovation; the UN Report (1993) points out that "in contrast to small and medium sized firms in general, not only do transnational small and medium sized firms conduct more R&D, but they produce more patented products."[16] Also, smaller firms with foreign affiliates have larger domestic market share, 30 percent of the market in their primary product, and their affiliates hold 38 percent of their markets. These large market shares and high R&D spending rates are consistent with smaller multinationals having innovative "edges."

*Caveat (ii): The Numbers May Be Misleading*

Small and medium-sized firms' disproportionately low share of foreign direct investment might be exaggerated. A multinational firm's operation is, by nature, greater in scale and scope. As a small firm builds up its foreign operation, it presumably quickly attains a size that qualifies it to be classified as a large firm.[17] Indeed, Vernon's (1966) product life-cycle theory posits that the diffusion of new products takes time. Information about a new product may reach domestic consumers first, causing domestic growth to precede international growth. Thus, a dearth of small firms among multinationals does not mean small firms will not expand abroad.

Despite these caveats, smaller firms may well be less likely to move into foreign markets than larger firms. There are two broad classes of reasons for this.

*(a) Barriers to Entry in Foreign Expansions Are Probably Higher for Smaller Firms*

Each of the barriers to entry we discussed previously in this essay that limit the scope for expansion of smaller firms is probably an even greater obstruction when international expansion is contemplated.

The same shortcomings of financial institutions and markets that we argued might prevent innovative small firms from growing rapidly would present even greater barriers to foreign expansion. If a small U.S. company cannot get a bank loan to expand domestically, it is unlikely locating the collateral abroad would improve the firm's creditworthiness. Moreover, if a country's banks will not lend to a small domestic firm, it is unlikely foreign banks would. Consistent with this, among firms with foreign operations, small and medium-sized firms tend to have partially owned foreign affiliates while large firms have fully owned affiliates. Only 47 percent of small firms' foreign affiliates are wholly owned, compared to 53 percent for large firms.[18] Also, 26 percent of small and medium-sized firms' foreign expansions take the form of joint ventures, versus 17 percent for large firms. Nevertheless, they are consistent with capital constraints disproportionately affecting smaller multinationals.

If lack of information about how labor, input, and product markets work is a barrier to domestic expansion, as we argued before, it is a blockade against foreign expansion. Organizing production and marketing in foreign countries is even harder than doing so domestically for a new firm. The entering firm has to work with a new legal system, bureaucratic regime, and set of social customs. It must hire and manage a labor force accustomed to the local economy. It must send out expatriate managers and experts. Evans et al. (1991) find that initial foreign expansions are often thwarted by suboptimal management. Simply put, managers inexperienced in foreign direct investment may not have the necessary knowledge to be efficient international operators.

As we argued previously, larger firms have inherent advantages in overcoming artificial barriers to entry. They can afford more delays, lawyers, campaign contributions, and other bribes. De Soto (1989) and others argue that artificial entry barriers, especially those maximally impregnable barriers due to government, are more pervasive in developing countries. Smaller multinationals do indeed concentrate their foreign direct investment in developed countries, although this could also be consistent with their having less information about more exotic countries.[19]

*(b) Many Foreign Markets Offer Poor Protection for Property Rights*

The key advantage smaller firms have over larger firms as vehicles for innovation is the better protection of innovators' property rights the former offer. Perversely, this importance of property rights over innovations may be critical in limiting small innovative firms' overseas expansion. Shleifer and Vishny (1993), DeSoto (1989), and others argue that poorly protected property rights are a pervasive problem in many developing countries. This is especially true for property rights over intangible assets like patents, trademarks, and so forth.[20]

A firm that expands into a country that offers no real recourse against the theft of such assets will risk setting up competitors that otherwise would not be viable. Yet these intangible assets are precisely the things that might make international expansion desirable in the first place for the small firms that own them. Since property rights are least protected in developing countries, this might also explain the preference of small multinationals for operations in other developed economies.

In contrast, the sorts of intangibles larger multinationals might bring, things like managerial, production, or marketing expertise, may be harder to steal, rendering international expansion by larger firms relatively more attractive. Also, large firms might have more credibility in threatening foreign governments and companies with retaliation when their patents or trademarks are stolen.

Therefore, the disadvantages that keep small firms small in domestic markets are likely to have similar or stronger effects in keeping them from expanding abroad, and the key advantage of smaller firms as vehicles for innovation, their better protection of innovators' property rights, becomes less clear-cut when foreign expansion might put those property rights at risk in underdeveloped or corrupt legal systems.[21]

## Intermediated Expansion via Larger Multinational Enterprises

In principle, one might imagine small start-up firms creating new ideas and then slowly developing into large, capital-rich firms as they market their products on a steadily larger scale. This is the thrust of the corporate life cycle outlined by Jovanovic (1982). The modern global economy of the 1990s, however, leads us to a new course; there is now a symbiotic relationship between small and large firms in the creative destruction process.

Global competition makes larger firms pay closer attention to innovations available with a view toward buying or applying them. Large firms often rely heavily on support groups of suppliers and other vertically related alliances. For example, the competitiveness of big automobile manufacturers depends critically on the efficiency of their parts suppliers. The success of many high-tech firms depends on a large pool of independent scientists and free-lance software writers. In many ways, large multinationals compete on the strength of their supporting casts as much as on their own strengths (Gomes-Casseres 1996).

The implication is that large multinational firms often serve as international conduits for the innovations of smaller firms.[22] Global competition induces multinationals to source from the most efficient suppliers worldwide. When multinationals purchase an input from an innovative supplier in one country for use through its international operations, they are essentially applying that supplier's innovation worldwide. Yet, the supplier need not expand abroad directly. Indirect international diffusion of this sort makes innovative suppliers more profitable. Because of the greater scale and scope of multinational firms' global markets, the small innovative support firms can earn greater returns, and they do not even have to spend resources to overcome barriers against international expansion themselves! The existence of successful multinational firms therefore encourages innovation by smaller firms. Aitken, Hanson, and Harrison (1994) present evidence that multinational firms do in fact induce more exports by smaller firms.

Moreover, industries that are vertically related to multinationals compete internationally even though they have no direct investment or even sales abroad; the competition takes place as the multinationals compete. Direct international competition between supporting industries in different countries is not necessary to bring about efficiency improvements. Chung, Mitchell, and Yeung (1994) show that U.S. automobile parts makers became more productive as competition between U.S. and Japanese auto assemblers increased. They argue that heightened international competition downstream increased the penalties on "unfit" suppliers, and they either improved or did not survive.

This sort of intermediary role for multinationals need not be confined to vertically related suppliers. Independent smaller firms with a new final product might find using multinational firms as intermediary agent in global marketing more efficient than breaking into foreign markets directly. Multinational firms have existing networks of global affiliates and established marketing skills. Distributing the innovation internationally via a multinational firm means giving that firm a cut, and so reducing the ultimate return from foreign sales, yet it calls for very little investment in building up foreign organizational and distribution infrastructure. Highly innovative garment producers and footwear producers in the Far East got rich this way. In the process, they displaced many less efficient producers in North America and elsewhere.[23]

Sometimes, the greatest synergy might be achieved through continual mergers of new small firms with innovative products into large firms with international market access. Thus, highly innovative small pharmaceutical companies are continuously absorbed into larger multinationals as the industry is forced to become more efficient. Williamson (1975, 205–6, emphasis added) has also noted the inherent tension between hierarchical bureaucratic organizations and entrepreneurial activity. He concluded:

> I am to regard the early stage innovative disabilities of large size as serious and propose the following hypothesis: An efficient procedure by which to introduce new products is for the initial development and market testing to be performed by independent inventors and small firms (perhaps new entrants) in an industry, *the successful development then to be acquired, possibly through licensing or merger, for subsequent marketing by a larger multidivision enterprise.*[24]

Larger firms thus act as catalysts, or facilitators, allowing smaller firms to expand internationally by proxy. Indeed, given the list of reasons for small innovative firms to forgo foreign expansion, indirect access to foreign markets via multinationals might well be the efficient choice. Small firms need not expand internationally themselves for the world economy to benefit fully from their innovations. They need only supply multinationals, which then serve as the intermediator of the international diffusion of small firms' innovations.

There are two drawbacks to the intermediated modes of foreign expansion. First, there are transaction difficulties. Innovations are often information-based. Transactions of innovations will face the usual agency problem and the information asymmetry problem ("market for lemon problem"). Also, the small firm has to be concerned that its transaction partner, the large multinational firm, will hijack its innovation. Moreover, commercializing an innovation involves investing in specific assets. The small innovating firm may be concerned that the multinational firm extracts ex post its rightful earnings by hold-up means.

Transaction problems are mitigated by designing mutually incentive compatible contracts. A government can reduce transaction difficulties by establishing and enforcing a transparent and reliable contractual regime. For example, by raising the punishment on legal contractual violations, a government makes commitment to legal contract more credible and thus makes legal contracts a more useful tool to formulate incentive compatible contracts.

Another drawback to the intermediated modes of international expansion is that large multinational firms may have bargaining power over small innovative firms. For instance, if a single large multinational is the monopoly supplier of access to world markets for smaller firms in a given country, region, or industry, it could extract monopoly rents and inhibit innovation. A large number of competing multinationals would insure that indirect access to foreign markets for smaller firms is efficiently priced. This consideration suggests that we need open competition both globally and in the home country (Morck and Yeung 1995).

## Policy Implications

We have argued that many small and medium-sized firms are initiators of Schumpeterian innovations. The optimum rate of international diffusion of these innovations enhances global welfare.

Small and medium-sized firms' observed low rate of direct international expansion often leads to suggestions about giving them special policy help.[25] We urge caution. First, as we have pointed out earlier, the observed home-boundedness of small and medium-sized firms may be exaggerated due to data definition. Also, many small and medium-sized firms are local niche players undertaking no innovation activities. Policy favoritism toward them should be for the redistribution objective, with little obvious help toward efficiency improvement.

Second, as we have argued in the previous section, the internationalization of small and medium-sized firms' innovations can be intermediated by large multinationals, not just via direct international expansion by small and medium-sized firms. With its presence, there is no presumption that there is too little international diffusion of small and medium-sized firms' innovation, even when direct international expansion by small and medium-sized firms is truly taking place at an extraordinarily low rate.

Still, the policy assumption that there is too little international diffusion of small and medium-sized firms' innovation appears plausible, particularly in consideration of the formidable entry barriers we mentioned earlier. While we shall proceed with the assumption, we emphasize that the fundamental question whether we have too little or too much creative destruction is unresolved, a point we address in our concluding section.

Accepting the current policy assumption, we raise two categories of policy questions: (1) Is the private sector systematically making the wrong choice between the direct and intermediated mode of international expansion? If so, what needs to be done? (2) What should be the policy guidelines to improve the overall rate of international diffusion by SMEs' innovation?

There are three sets of costs fundamental to the choice between the direct and the intermediated mode of international expansion. The first set of costs is associated with entry barriers and protection of property rights. In the direct mode, smaller firms must each build up an organizational and tangible-asset infrastructure to support international operations. As well, they must each separately pay the costs of becoming efficient operators in global markets. All these costs stem from the need to overcome entry barriers and to protect property rights. In the intermediated mode, there will be savings on these costs because multinational firms already have established their international networks and are more able to protect property rights. In other words, in direct international expansion, the expanding small and medium-sized firm incurs some socially redundant investment.

The second set of costs is the transactions costs incurred in the intermediated mode of international expansion. We have mentioned in the previous section that in the intermediated mode of foreign expansion, there are transaction difficulties between a small and medium-sized firm and its intermediator. To counter transaction difficulties, the transaction partners must spend resources to develop an incentive compatible contract and spend resources to make the contract credible, for example, making credible pre-commitments and spending on monitoring. These are nontrivial costs. Also, the second-best nature of incentive compatible contracts, as a resolution to transaction difficulties, implies that the value created in intermediated foreign expansion may be less, ceteris paribus, than that created in direct foreign expansion.

The third cost arises when the intermediator has market power in serving to internationally diffuse the small and medium-sized firm's innovation. The intermediator then will extract rents from the small firm; this cost is a transfer from the small firm to the intermediating multinational.

Assume that a small firm develops an innovation that would have value in international markets. In the direct mode of international expansion, the cost of going overseas, from the social perspective, is the small firm's investment in the market entry and property rights protection. In the intermediated mode, again from the social perspective, the cost is the large firm's investment in the market entry and property rights protection and the deadweight loss due to transaction difficulties between the large and the small firm. Hence, the optimal social choice between the two modes of international expansion depends on the savings in the market entry costs and property rights protection costs in the intermediated mode and the deadweight transaction cost incurred in the same mode. When the former exceeds the latter, the intermediated mode of international expansion should be chosen over the direct mode.

In making its private choice, the small and medium-sized firm will opt for the intermediated mode if the associated savings in market entry costs and property rights protection costs exceeds the deadweight transaction costs and the rent extraction by the intermediating large firm. The small firm's maximum receipt from the intermediating large firm is the potential value of the innovation on international markets minus the large firm's spending on market entry and property rights protection and the deadweight loss transaction costs. The actual receipt is the difference minus the rents extracted by the intermediating large firm. The difference between the small firm's earnings in intermediated and direct international expansion then is equal to the savings on market entry and protection of property rights minus the deadweight transactions costs and the rents extracted by the intermediating firm.

Hence, the private choice between the two modes of international expansion is socially efficient as long as rent extraction by the intermediating firm in the intermediated mode is zero. If rent extraction by the intermediator is nontrivial, the private market will choose direct international expansion more often than it should, leading to too much redundant investment in market entry and protection of property rights. This reveals that the first and foremost policy guidelines should be to mitigate rent extraction and to resist policies in favor of helping small and medium-sized firms to expand internationally.

The policy concern should go beyond just correcting potentially wrong private market choice between the direct and the intermediated modes of international expansion. If the rate of creative destruction is indeed too low, public policies should also aim to increase the creation and international diffusion of innovations by small firms. The preceding analyses suggest that policies should aim to reduce the costs in international expansion. That is, policies should aim to reduce private market costs incurred for the protection of property rights, to reduce entry barriers, and to reduce transactions costs.

The analysis also suggests that policy subsidies to help small and medium-sized firms to expand overseas will lead to excess direct international expansion. Such policy measures reduce the small firm's market entry and protection of property rights costs. They thus reduce the beneficial savings in market entry and property rights protection costs when intermediated international expansion is chosen over direct international expansion. As a consequence, direct international expansion is chosen too often, leading to excess redundant investment in market entry and property rights protection undertaken via small firms.

## Conclusion

In this essay we have argued that small firms are indeed the engines of global economic growth. Creative destruction plays an important role in the process of economic growth. Small firms play a crucial role in the process of creative destruction because the diffusion of property rights, along with bureaucratic inertia and other problems characteristic of large firms, dampen potential innovators' incentives to be creative. Thus, we argue that smaller firms are better at creating radical innovations because they better protect the innovator's property rights.

The continued ability of start-up companies to challenge industry leaders is a critical public policy issue. However, there has been a lack of solid public policy analysis on the subject of public policy toward small firms. A theme of this essay has been the relative advantage of *direct* versus *intermediated* international expansion by small and medium-sized firms. We raise several conceptual considerations important in comparing the two modes of international expansion.

What is at the disposal of policymakers is the ability to either increase or reduce the speed of creative destruction and therefore the rate of economic growth through creative public policy. As we have suggested, those policies include: the elimination of as many barriers to entry as possible; protecting innovators' property rights; maintaining an efficient institutional environment to mitigate transaction costs; and opening domestic markets to multinationals.

The role of government can be stated simply. Government policies that *weaken* property rights or strengthen barriers to entry slow the process of creative destruction. Government policies that *strengthen* property rights or lower entry barriers speed it up.

What is the socially optimal rate of creative destruction? Is more innovation always better? Ready access to global markets increases the returns to innovation and therefore the incentive to innovate. Rapid innovation, in turn, leads to further globalization as firms seek greater economies of scale on which to apply their innovations. This positive feedback spiral is the motive force behind the emerging global economy.

An increased rate of innovation is good in that it reduces production costs and/or increases consumer choice. These societal gains stem from the "creative" side of creative destruction. More rapid innovation is bad in that it can make existing physical and human capital obsolete. In doing this it can disrupt careers and communities. These societal costs stem from the "destructive" side of creative destruction.

No well-accepted theory of a socially optimal rate of creative destruction currently exists. Many economists writing about the increased pace of innovation and the rise of the global economy immediately assume more innovation is socially good. This view is presumably shared by firms that lobby for R&D subsidies and by the branches of government that grant them. While this view may well be right, it is important to recognize that there is no compelling economic theory backing this up.

The decision as to the optimal rate of creative destruction is essentially political. The policy recommendations we have made would enhance the positive feedback spiral of increasing innovation and globalization. If this is viewed as socially undesirable, these recommendations should instead be viewed as proscriptions.

## NOTES

We wish to thank Lee Preston, Frank Stafford, and seminar participants at the October 1995 CIBER conference on Small and Medium Sized Enterprises (SMEs) and the Global Economy, at the University of Maryland, and the sixth conference of the

International Joseph A. Schumpeter Society, Stockholm, Sweden, June 1996, for helpful comments. All errors and omissions remain our responsibility.

1. For a review of the literature on small firms see Acs 1995 and 1996 and Storey 1994.

2. Acs and Audretsch 1988, 683. Among large firms, the correlation coefficient is 0.107; that among smaller firms is twice as large. The measure of innovation activities is the number of innovations in each four-digit SIC industry recorded in 1982. Innovation is defined as "a process that begins with an invention, proceeds with the development of the invention, and results in the introduction of a new product, process, or services to the market place."

3. Acs and Audretsch 1988, 687.

4. This is true at least in those industries where information asymmetries create a divergence of opinion about the value of new knowledge. If the information is undervalued agents may have to take it outside of the organization.

5. See Shleifer 1995.

6. In some corporations, employees have to sign agreements in which they surrender the property rights to their inventions to the firm.

7. Acs and Audretsch 1988, 687, table 7.

8. At the 1995 White House Conference on Small Business, of the sixty public policy issues cited, access to capital was the one most frequently mentioned (U.S. Small Business Administration 1995).

9. See Lerner 1994 and 1995.

10. Capital market imperfections are a special case of this more general information problem. Investors are unwilling to buy into firms about which they know little.

11. Acs and Audretsch (1989) obtained empirical evidence that concentration deters the entry of small firms, but apparently does not impede the entry of larger firms.

12. "In a Polish Shipyard, Signals of Eastern Europe's Revival—Medium size companies are the engines of a region's growth," *New York Times,* July 4, 1995. See Loveman and Johnson 1995.

13. In Italy in 1982, small and medium-sized enterprises' (SMEs') share of establishment is 96.9 percent and share of employment is 53.4 percent, but its share of multinational enterprises (MNEs) is only 28.7 percent and its share of MNEs' foreign employment is only 7.4 percent, even in 1987. In Sweden, SMEs' share of establishment in 1988 is 97.5 percent, its share of employment is 63.4 percent, while its share of MNE establishment is 74 percent and its share of MNE foreign employment is merely 2 percent. In UK, SMEs' share of establishment is 98.4 percent (in 1981) but its share of MNE establishment is only 25 percent.

14. UN Report 1993, 53.

15. Ibid., 21.

16. Ibid., 97.

17. The UN definition of a large firm is above 500 employees in manufacturing, above 100 in wholesaling, and above 50 employees in retailing and services.

18. UN Report 1993, 83.

19. Ibid., 51, table III.1.

20. SMEs are less likely to file for patents abroad than large businesses across all technology areas. When only the highest-value patents within each technology area are considered, a smaller proportion of SMEs' patents is still filed abroad in the majority

of technology areas. Small and large business patents that are filed abroad, however, are quite similar in the number of countries in which applications are filed. This suggests that SMEs with valuable inventions face special barriers in obtaining foreign patent protection because of limited resources (Mogee 1996).

21. Intellectual property protection was the most frequently cited international policy recommendation at the 1995 White House Conference on Small Business (U.S. Small Business Administration 1995)

22. Large multinational firms can also serve as conduits for circumventing market fragmentation of various sorts. It is well known that trade barriers stimulate foreign direct investment. Canada's "National Policy" of high tariffs early this century exploited this to create an economy of subsidiaries. Multinational firms can also bypass capital market controls and other restrictions.

23. Foreign direct investment appears to augment home and host country productivity, and this appears to be due to both technology diffusion and increased competitive pressure. See Blomström and Persson 1983, Blomström 1986, Caves 1974, and Chung, Mitchell, and Yeung 1994.

24. Many large multidivisional firms are also multinational.

25. UN Conference on Trade and Development Program on Transnational Corporations—Small and Medium Sized Transnational Corporations: Role, Impact and Policy Implications, 1993.

## REFERENCES

Acs, Zoltan J., ed. 1995. "Symposium on Harrison's 'Lean and Mean.' " *Small Business Economics* 7 (5): 333–63.

———. 1996. *Small Firms and Economic Growth.* Vols. 1 and 2. Cheltenham, U.K.: Edward Elgar Publishers.

Acs, Zoltan J., and David B. Audretsch. 1988. "Innovation in Large and Small Firms: An Empirical Analysis." *American Economic Review* 78 (4): 678–90.

———. 1989. "Small-firm Entry in US Manufacturing." *Economica* 56:255–65.

———. 1991. *Innovation and Small Firms.* Cambridge: MIT Press.

Aitken, Brian, Gordon H. Hanson, and Ann E. Harrison. 1994. "Spillover, Foreign Investment, and Export Behavior." Working paper, Columbia University.

Audretsch, David B. 1995. *Innovation and Industry Evolution.* Cambridge: MIT Press.

Baumol, William J. 1990. "Entrepreneurship: Productive, Unproductive, and Destructive." *Journal of Political Economy* 98 (5): 893–921.

Blomström, Magnus. 1986. "Foreign Investment and Productive Efficiency: The Case of Mexico." *Journal of Industrial Economics* 35 (1): 97–110.

Blomström, Magnus, and Håkan Persson. 1983. "Foreign Investment and Spillover Efficiency in an Underdeveloped Economy: Evidence from the Mexican Manufacturing Industry." *World Development* 11 (6): 493–501.

Caves, Richard E. 1974. "Multinational Firms, Competition, and Productivity in Host-Country Markets." *Economica* 41:176–93.

Chung, Wilbur, Will Mitchell, and Bernard Yeung. 1994. "Foreign Direct Investment and Host Country Productivity: The Case of the American Automotive Components Industry." University of Michigan, Institute of Public Policy Studies and Department of Economics Discussion Paper No. 367.

Cockburn, Iain, and Rebecca Henderson. 1995. "Do Agency Costs Explain Variation in Innovative Performance." Working paper, Massachusetts Institute of Technology, presented at the NBER IO Summer Conference, Cambridge.

De Soto, Hernando. 1989. *The Other Path.* New York: Harper and Row.

Diamond, Douglas W. 1985. "Optimal Release of Information by Firms." *Journal of Finance* 40:1071–94.

———. 1989. "Reputation Acquisition in Debt Markets." *Journal of Political Economy* 97:828–67.

———. 1991. "Monitoring and Reputation: The Choice Between Bank Loans and Directly Placed Debt." *Journal of Political Economy* 99:689–721.

Evans, David S., and Boyan Jovanovic. 1989. "An Estimated Model of Entrepreneurial Choice under Liquidity Constraints." *Journal of Political Economy* 97 (4): 808–27.

Evans, Wendy, Henry Lane, and Shawna O'Grady. 1991. *Border Crossings: Doing Business in the U.S.* Scarborough, Ontario: Prentice Hall Canada.

Fujita, Masataka. 1995. "Small and Medium Sized Transnational Corporations: Trends and Patterns of Foreign Direct Investment." *Small Business Economics* 7 (3): 183–204.

Gomes-Casseres, Benjamin. 1996. *The Alliance Revolution: The New Shape of Business Rivalry.* Cambridge: Harvard University Press.

Holtz-Eakin, Douglas, David Joulfaian, and Harvey S. Rosen. 1994a. "Entrepreneurial Decisions and Liquidity Constraints." *Rand Journal of Economics* 25 (2): 334–47.

———. 1994b. "Sticking It Out: Entrepreneurial Survival and Liquidity Constraints." *Journal of Political Economy* 102 (1): 53–75.

Jovanovic, Boyan. 1982. "Selection and the Evolution of Industry." *Econometrica* 50:649–70.

King, Robert G., and Ross Levine. 1993. "Finance and Growth: Schumpeter Might Be Right." *Quarterly Journal of Economics* 108:717–37.

Klitgaard, Robert. 1990. *Tropical Gangsters.* New York: Basic Books.

Lenway, Stefanie, Randall Morck, and Bernard Yeung. 1996. "Rent-Seeking, Protectionism and Innovation in the American Steel Industry." *Economic Journal* 106 (435): 410–21.

Lerner, Josh. 1994. "Venture Capitalists and the Decision to Go Public." *Journal of Financial Economics* 35:293–316.

———. 1995. "Venture Capitalists and the Oversight of Private Firms." *Journal of Finance* 50:301–18.

Loveman, Gary, and Simon Johnson. 1995. *Starting Over in Eastern Europe: Entrepreneurship and Economic Renewal.* Cambridge: Harvard Business School Press.

Mogee, Mary E. 1996. "Foreign Patenting Behavior of Small and Large Firms." Prepared for the U.S. Small Business Administration Office of Advocacy under Contract No. SBA-8140-OA-94.

Morck, Randall, and Bernard Yeung. 1991. "Why Investors Value Multinationality." *Journal of Business* 46 (2): 165–87.

———. 1995. "The Future of Foreign-Owned Subsidiaries in Canada." In *Corporate Decision Making and Governance in Canada,* ed. Ron Daniels and Randall Morck. Industry Canada, Canadian Government Printing Office.

Murphy, Kevin M., Andrei Shleifer, and Robert W. Vishny. 1993. "Why Is Rent-Seeking Costly to Growth?" *American Economic Review* 82 (2): 409–14.

National Academy of Engineering. 1995. *Risk and Innovation.* Washington, DC: National Academy Press.

Newbould, G. D., Peter Buckley, and J. C. Thurwell. 1978. *Going International: The Experiences of Smaller Companies Overseas.* New York: Wiley and Sons.

Nugent, Jeffrey B. 1996. "What Explains the Trend Reversal in the Size Distribution of Korean Manufacturing Establishments." *Journal of Development Economics* 48:225–51.

Petersen, Mitchell A., and Raghuman G. Ragan. 1994. "The Benefits of Lending Relationships: Evidence from Small Business Data." *Journal of Finance* 49:3–37.

Schumpeter, Joseph A. 1934. *The Theory of Economic Development.* Cambridge, MA: Harvard University Press.

———. 1942. *Capitalism, Socialism and Democracy.* New York: Harper and Row.

Shaver, Myles, Will Mitchell, and Bernard Yeung. 1995. "The Effect of Own-Firm and Other-Firm Experience on Foreign Direct Investment Survival in the United States, 1987–1992." Working paper, Stern School, New York University.

Shleifer, Andrei. 1995. "Establishing Property Rights." Harvard University, mimeo.

Shleifer, Andrei, and Robert W. Vishny. 1993. "Corruption." *Quarterly Journal of Economics* 108 (3): 599–617.

Storey, David. 1994. *Understanding the Small Business Sector.* London: Routledge.

Thurik, Roy. 1996. "Small Firms, Entrepreneurship and Economic Growth." In *Small Business in the Modern Economy,* ed. Piet Hein Admiraal. F. de Vries Lectures.

UN Conference on Trade and Development Program on Transnational Corporations. 1993. *Small and Medium-Sized Transnational Corporations: Role, Impact and Policy Implications.* New York: United Nations.

United States Small Business Administration. 1995. "Foundations for a New Century." The White House Conference on Small Business Commission, Washington, DC.

Vernon, Raymond. 1966. "International Investment and International Trade in the Product Cycle." *Quarterly Journal of Economics* 81:190–207.

Williamson, Oliver E. 1975. *Markets and Hierarchies: Antitrust Analysis and Implications.* New York: Free Press.

# Alliance Strategies of Small Firms

*Benjamin Gomes-Casseres*

Students of international business have traditionally believed that success in foreign markets required large size. Small firms were thought to be at a disadvantage compared to larger firms, because of the fixed costs of learning about foreign environments, communicating at long distances, and negotiating with national governments. These costs "constitute an important reason for expecting that foreign investment will be mainly an activity of large firms," argued Richard Caves (1982) in his comprehensive review of the literature on the multinational enterprise.

A number of empirical studies seemed to back up this conclusion. Thomas Horst (1972) found that after controlling for industry effects, the only factor significantly affecting the propensity of firms to invest abroad was their size. Raymond Vernon (1970) found that technological advantages were important in firms' propensity to invest abroad, but that these advantages were often correlated with scale. More recently, Alfred Chandler's exhaustive historical research concluded that "to compete globally you have to be big" (1990).

So what was a small firm to do? Common sense gave one answer: Seek help! Biotechnology firms seemed to follow this advice as they sought out alliances with large pharmaceutical firms to commercialize their inventions. So did semiconductor and software firms that sought investments and support from computer giants. Both Intel and Microsoft got their head start in the personal computer business through their early alliances with IBM. For these firms, key partnerships made up for lack of scale. In the terminology introduced by Acs et al. (1997), alliances are an "intermediated" form of international business by small firms—they rely on larger partners to give them the scale and scope often required for success abroad.

But not all small firms followed this prescription. A substantial number did the opposite—they refused to share their technologies and insisted on going it alone. In a survey of seven small U.S. firms that were successful in international markets, Tomás Kohn and I found a much lower share of joint ventures and licensing than one might have expected based on the traditional view previously described (see description of sample in Gomes-Casseres and Kohn forthcoming). Of the thirty-six foreign investments of these firms, only five (14 percent) were jointly owned with local firms; by comparison, the share of joint ventures for large U.S. firms has historically hovered at over 30 percent (Gomes-Casseres 1988). Of the foreign ventures in our sample, 92 percent were majority-owned by the U.S. parent, compared to 86 percent of the total population of firms in the U.S. Commerce Department's 1989 Benchmark Survey (1992). Finally, the firms in our sample had only seven licensing arrangements with foreign firms; and one firm accounted for six of these. However we turned the data, one conclusion seemed inescapable: our firms formed fewer—not more—alliances than one might have expected, given the preceding arguments. Why?

This essay addresses three questions that follow from these observations. First, when do some small firms use alliances to do business abroad? In the next section, I will propose an answer that may also help clarify other issues regarding small firms in international business. Second, how do small firms use alliances? The small firms that use alliances appear to mimic the in-house configuration and sets of capabilities deployed by their larger rivals. And third, what effects do the alliances of small firms have on their competitive performance? The potential for success, it turns out, is high, but so are the risks of failure.

The arguments in this essay are based on my reading of the literature and on ten years of empirical and theoretical research on alliances; they build on the discussion and evidence in Gomes-Casseres 1996. In addition, I use some results from research on small firms conducted jointly with Tomás Kohn. Data and examples will be cited to clarify the arguments, but no attempt will be made to present conclusive tests; on the contrary, this essay is meant to generate discussion and open up avenues for future research.

## Competitive Strategies of Small Firms

The observations just cited suggest that the propensity of small firms to use alliances might be bimodally distributed—some of them have a higher-than-average propensity to collaborate with others, and others, a lower-than-average propensity. No aggregate data exists to show this, but the previous literature and anecdotal and small-sample evidence point in this direction. As is often the case with bimodal distributions, this pattern may indicate that the population of small firms contains two different subgroups. If so, what might be the distinguishing characteristics of these subgroups?

As a first cut, the key difference between these subgroups may be the *size of the firm relative to its rivals.* In a given population of small firms—where "small" is defined by absolute scale of, for example, employment, assets, or sales—there will be some firms that are smaller than other firms in their market, and others that are larger than their rivals. Another way of putting this is that a firm may be large or small for its market, regardless of its absolute size. Many small firms, in fact, are large players in their niche—they occupy dominant market positions and outflank their rivals in terms of resources and capabilities. Other small firms are tiny compared to their rivals, occupying second- or third-tier positions in their markets.

Relative size is a key factor behind any firm's alliance strategy, regardless of their absolute size. Studies of ownership strategies among *Fortune 500* firms showed that second-tier firms tended to form more joint ventures than first-tier firms (Stopford and Wells 1972). In industry after industry, dominant firms—which by definition are large for their market—tend to shun alliances, whereas weaker firms use alliances to shore up their capabilities. In contrast, lagging firms—even when they are large by other measures—tend to use alliances to catch up with leaders (Gomes-Casseres 1996).

The logic of alliance formation for firms that are much smaller in absolute scale is no different. They too, tend to seek alliances when they are small relative to their rivals and shun alliances when they dominate their rivals. To see why, we need to examine two things: (1) the typical business strategies of the two subgroups of so-called small firms and (2) the general motivations behind alliance formation. I will take up the second question first.

## Context, Capabilities, and Control

I define alliances broadly as an administrative arrangement to govern an *incomplete contract* between *separate firms* in which each partner has *limited control.* These arrangements can take different forms—from joint ventures, to joint R&D programs, to cooperative marketing arrangements—but each aims to govern joint decision making among the partners. I also define a new unit of competition called a *constellation*—a set of firms linked together through alliances. These constellations can consist of any number of allied firms, from pairs to triads to groups of various sizes. Regardless of their size and composition, however, these constellations compete with other constellations as well as with traditional single firms.

Three factors determine when constellations arise and how they compete: capabilities, control, and context. By *capabilities,* I mean the set of tangible and intangible assets that enable an organization to develop, make, and market goods and services. *Control* stands for the authority of a decision maker in using and deploying these capabilities. And *context* refers to the

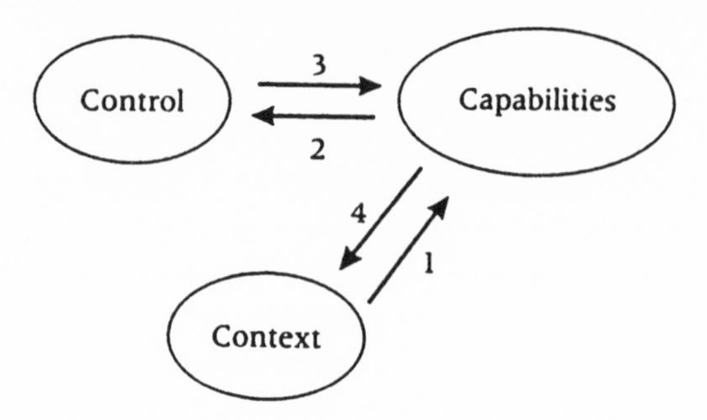


**Fig. 1. Determinants of alliance strategies**

environment that places demands and creates opportunities for the organization. In this framework, firms and constellations are different ways of controlling a set of capabilities. The single firm has full control over all its capabilities; in the constellation, control over the set of capabilities of the group is shared among separate firms. Furthermore, constellations typically differ in the way they control capabilities; the pattern of alliances inside a constellation creates and determines the allocation of control.

Some simple relationships among the three factors are indicated in figure 1. The context of an organization often determines the capabilities that it needs to be successful (arrow 1). If a firm has these capabilities internally, it need not form an alliance; otherwise, it might seek one. In either case, therefore, the set of capabilities needed influences the structure of control in the organization (arrow 2). This structure of control, in turn, influences the way the capabilities are managed, and the degree and type of investments made to upgrade the capabilities over time (arrow 3). As the set of capabilities changes in response to these investments, the organization might offer new products and services; this may transform the pattern of competition and the context facing other players in the industry (arrow 4).

This framework is applicable to firms of all sizes. It also helps us define more precisely what we mean by *relatively small* firms, the kind of firm that tends to have a higher-than-average propensity to form alliances. The determining factor in our framework is not size, but the competitive demands imposed by the environment—the capabilities required to succeed in a given context. In contexts with high economies of scale or scope, therefore, the most successful firms will tend to be larger than their rivals, all else equal. Firms that are smaller than their rivals will then seek alliances to increase their scale and scope. In other words, what matters is the size of the firm relative to the optimum in an industry.

From this perspective, firms that are smaller than their rivals need not always be at a disadvantage. Picture, for example, an industry that has long enjoyed economies of scale and in which the largest firms are dominant. Historically, therefore, relatively small firms in this industry have been at a disadvantage and can be expected to have used alliances to shore up their capabilities. Now, imagine that a change in the context—say the emergence of a new technology—reduces the advantages of scale, or even generates temporary diseconomies of scale. At this point, the disadvantage of relatively small firms decreases or is reversed—their small size may allow them to succeed against their larger rivals, even without alliances. However, if scale becomes an advantage again, only the small firms that have grown substantially will survive a shakeout.

This scenario is perhaps what has been occurring in computers, and perhaps in pharmaceuticals. In both industries, scale and scope have traditionally been essential to success, and huge multinational firms dominated markets. But the rise of microelectronics and biotechnology suddenly created advantages for small, entrepreneurial firms and challenges for the large, bureaucratic incumbents. This window for small firms, however, did not remain open forever, as the large firms restructured themselves or the erstwhile small firms grew to exploit new economies of scale. Apple, Compaq, Microsoft, and Intel, for example, could enter the market and establish themselves when IBM's dominance in mainframes was more of a hindrance than a help in the PC business. But today, scale and scope help determine who will survive in the PC market.

These considerations suggest that we need to examine the competitive context and general business strategies of small firms to explain their alliance behavior. Firms in each of the two identified subgroups, in fact, follow radically different business strategies. The first type of firm relies on its own capabilities to exploit market niches; the second tries to succeed in a larger market by using alliances to reach the required scale and scope.

## Exploiting Niches

A traditional explanation for the success of small firms was that they chose their battles carefully. They focus on areas where there are either no scale economies or even some diseconomies of scale. In Edith Penrose's words (1959; 1980: 222–23):

> The productive opportunities of small firms are . . . composed of those interstices left open by the large firms which the small firms see and believe they can take advantage of. . . . [T]he nature of the inter-

> stices is determined by the kind of activity in which the larger firms specialize, leaving other opportunities open.

Previous studies of small firms investing abroad found patterns that seem consistent with this view (Hackett 1977; Newbould et al. 1978; Buckley et al. 1983). In Hackett's words, "Multinational firms typically concentrate on expansion into those markets that offer the greatest profit potential and knowingly bypass smaller market segments" (1977:11). He found, as did Mascarenhas (1986), that small firms often went abroad in order to avoid head-on competition with larger domestic rivals. Mascarenhas (1986) and Namiki (1988) also found that "follower" firms tended to be most successful internationally when they focused on specialty markets or products, where economies of scale were not critical. Sweeney (1970) and Vlachoutsikos (1989) described how the "low profile" of small firms gave them an advantage over larger firms in gaining concessions from host governments.

The first type of small firm thus competes in niche markets that were of minor interest to large firms. Because of their narrow bases of expertise, these firms would probably have found it easier to expand their business into new markets abroad than into new product markets at home. The move abroad, in other words, is not an afterthought but is quite important to these firms. Once operating abroad, the firms would inevitably face new demands from buyers and gain opportunities to draw on resources in foreign production sites. This, in turn, might lead to a learning process that would further deepen the firms' capabilities in their niche. Because of the firms' dependence on leadership in their product niche, they cannot afford to fall behind in any country, and so need to adapt to disparate country environments. Through this learning process—which may well be enhanced by the flat organizational structures typical of small firms—the firm becomes even more experienced and specialized.

The combination of narrow focus and depth of expertise in this type of firm led Kohn and me to call this a "deep niche" strategy (Gomes-Casseres and Kohn 1997). The behavior of the twelve firms in our sample was consistent with these arguments. Their business strategies were characterized by these three elements:

> *Market dominance.* The firms in our group were generally large relative to their direct competitors. They usually occupied strong—even dominant—positions within their narrow market niches and typically had few direct competitors. Two companies reported that they held approximately a 30 percent share of the U.S. market, while three others esti-

mated that they each held over 40 percent of the *world* market for their products. Other researchers working on related projects found similar patterns of market dominance by small firms originating in Canada (Niosi 1997), the United Kingdom (Buckley and Mirza 1997), and Japan (Ozawa 1997).

*Technological leadership.* The firms were also often technological leaders within their industries. We asked interviewees to rank their firms' relative technological position in the industry between one (absolute leader) and five (last follower). Eight of the twelve firms reported that they were absolute leaders and only one reported that it was a follower; the average score for this question was 1.6. A number of them learned from experience that they had to become and maintain technological leadership in their niches. One company, for example, entered the testing equipment business in the late 1940s, even though larger firms were already well established. It focused on specialized engineering, expanded its customer service network worldwide, and developed deep expertise in applications-specific fixtures and adapters. Today, the company has almost one-third of the U.S. market, and it continues to deepen its capabilities by spending over 7 percent of sales on R&D. As a result, it pioneered the use of digital test and measurement instruments.

*Producer-good focus.* A corollary to the specialty role of the small firms was that they usually sold producer goods to a limited group of industrial buyers. One manufacturer of aerosol valves, for example, reported that 80 percent of its sales were to 20 percent of its customers. Furthermore, many of its customers were themselves multinational firms buying similar types of valves in several countries. The valve producer, therefore, like other specialty suppliers in our group, did not need to invest in extensive distribution networks or advertising. Rather, its sales strategy consisted of maintaining a leadership position in technology and cost, and cultivating relationships with a handful of multinational buyers. Kohn (1988) found a concentration on producer goods in a larger sample of small firms and provides a detailed analysis of the reasons for this pattern.

The type of firm represented in our sample, therefore, relied on in-house capabilities to compete in a narrow market segment. Not only did they not need alliances, but they preferred not to share control over key resources and technologies with partners.

## Reaching for Scale and Scope

Mips Computer Systems was a very different type of small firm. It employed fewer than 1,000 people, yet chose to take on huge, well-established companies, including IBM and Hewlett-Packard (HP). And it did this in a field where production scale and market penetration were critical to commercial success—the reduced instruction-set computing (RISC) industry. On its own, Mips clearly did not stand a chance.

Mips managers concluded early on that they needed allies—not one, but many. The Mips constellation started small, but it soon included six semiconductor partners and countless systems vendors. Allies brought production capacity, market presence, technologies, and cash. In return, Mips provided a unique semiconductor design and it coordinated the activities of the constellation. This strategy implied a transformation of the unit of competition. Legally, Mips remained a small corporation. But, economically, it was part of a much larger whole; and it was this larger whole that competed against other firms and groups. Increasingly, the talk in the industry became one of how the Mips "camp" was faring versus the camps centered around other firms.

This strategy was mandated by the firm's context. Even though Mips was one of the pioneers in the field of RISC processors, the successful production and sale of these chips required large-scale operations. Because of these scale economies, it was clear that only a few of the six or seven RISC designs on the market in the early 1990s could survive in the long run. This also meant that those designs that gained the largest market share had the greatest chance of survival. Market share, in turn, depended on the availability of hardware systems and software applications. This combination of factors led to a fierce standards battle among the RISC firms in which scale, scope, and sponsorship were key.

In standards battles, the number of firms in a network and especially their combined share of the total market are critical. These numbers reflect the degree to which the standard has been accepted among potential sponsors (see also Cusumano, Mylonadis, and Rosenbloom 1992). Early in the RISC battle, for example, Sun Microsystems persuaded a large number of firms to sign on to its technology, because Sun was already dominant in technical workstations. As a start-up company, Mips had a more challenging task in attracting partners; but, after DEC, NEC, and other major firms joined its group, others followed. Still, the growth of the Mips network was more modest than that of Sun. In 1991, however, Mips tried to leap-frog Sun with its Advanced Computing Environment (ACE) initiative. Figure 2 shows the structure of the main RISC alliance groups in early 1992. As can

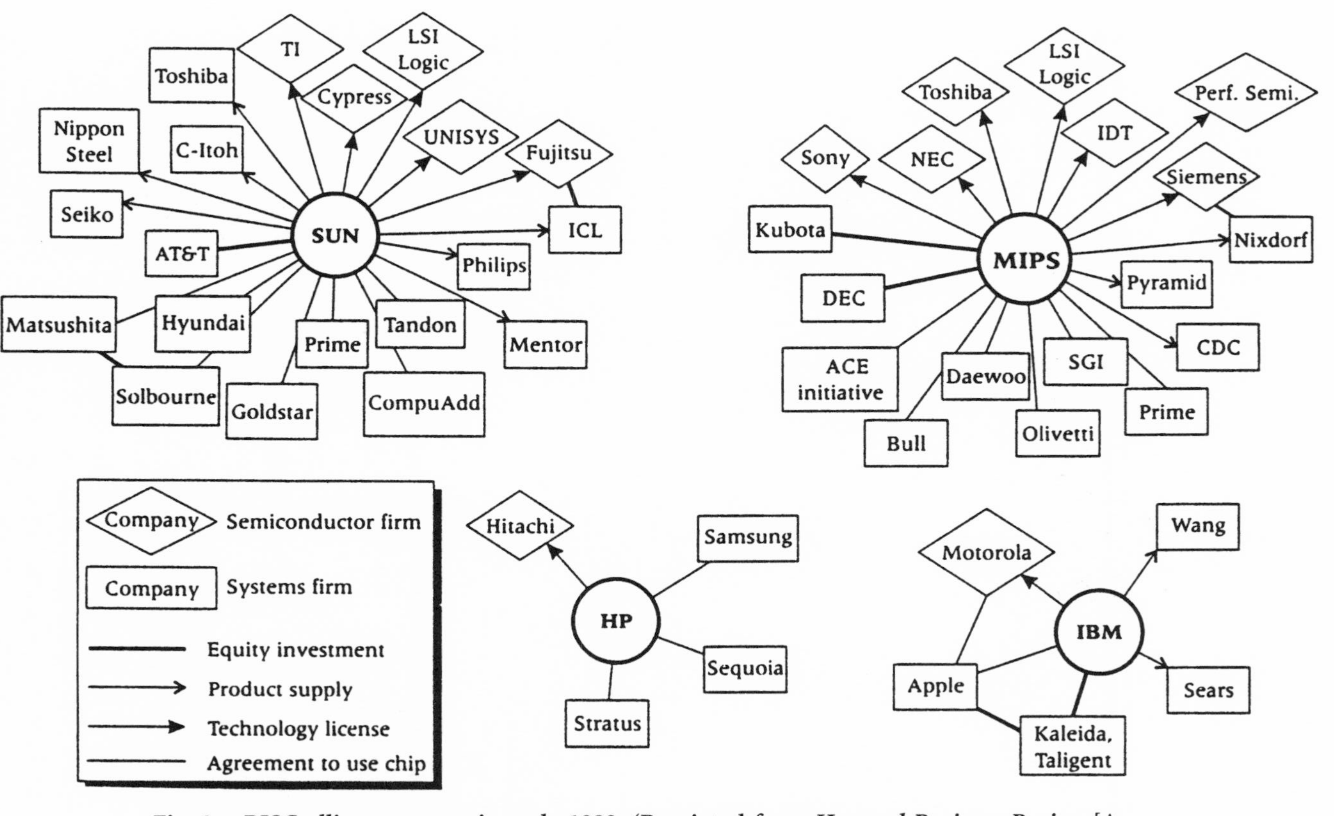


Fig. 2. RISC alliance groups in early 1992. (Reprinted from *Harvard Business Review* [An Exhibit] as Gomes-Casseres 1994. Copyright © 1994 by the President and Fellows of Harvard College; all rights reserved.)

be seen, the large firms in this battle—IBM and HP—also used alliances to spread their standards, but they relied much less on their partners than Mips and Sun.

Mips and Sun thus used allies to reach the scale, scope, and market impact that they could never hope to achieve on their own. "Because of the NEC connection," explained one Mips executive, "we are almost bigger than life in Japan." Central to this strategy, however, was a view of competition in which constellations—groups of firms—do battle with each other, not just firm against firm. Only as part of such a constellation could the small firms hope to succeed.

Several measures of size can be used to illustrate how the Mips and Sun groups attempted to reach the scale and scope of their larger rivals, IBM and HP. Table 1 shows these measures.

The table shows that in the semiconductor portion of the business, the Mips and Sun constellations produced more RISC chips in 1992 than did the IBM and HP groups; this advantage was partly a result of the late start by the latter two groups. Even so, Mips and Sun had more semiconductor

**Table 1. Market Presence and Production Scale of RISC Groups, ca. 1992**

| | Mips | Sun | HP | IBM |
|---|---|---|---|---|
| **Semiconductor business** | | | | |
| *RISC chips shipped (1992)* | | | | |
| Thousand units | 331 | 295 | 64 | 67 |
| Number of suppliers | 7 | 5 | 1 | 1 |
| Share of lead firm[a] (%) | 0 | 0 | 100 | 100 |
| *Total semiconductor production (1991)* | | | | |
| U.S. $ (in billions) | 14.5 | 11.7 | 5.0[b] | 10.0[b] |
| Number of suppliers | 6 | 7 | 2 | 2 |
| Share of lead firm[a] (%) | 0 | 0 | 10[b] | 60[b] |
| **Systems business** | | | | |
| *RISC workstation revenues (1992)* | | | | |
| U.S. $ (in billions) | 2.1 | 3.0 | 1.8 | 1.5 |
| Number of suppliers | 7 | 5 | 2 | 1 |
| Share of lead firm[a] % | 0 | 92 | 95 | 100 |
| *Total microcomputer revenues (1991)* | | | | |
| U.S. $ (in billions) | 5.5 | 7.3 | 2.2 | 15.4 |
| Number of suppliers | 8 | 11 | 2 | 5 |
| Share of lead firm[a] (%) | 0 | 24 | 46 | 47 |

*Source:* RISC semiconductor and systems data from Dataquest; other data from Dataquest and Gartner Group. The table includes only the members of each group for which data were available; data on the most important members were available for all groups.

[a]"Lead firm" refers to the firms in the column headings.

[b]Estimated, as most of this production is captive and not reported.

partners, and the combined production of these partners was larger than that of the IBM and HP partners. But note that Mips itself did not make *any* semiconductors.

Total semiconductor production is also a relevant measure of size in this case, because investments in process technology, equipment, and human resources could often be shared between different types of semiconductor devices. For example, even though NEC produced only 110,000 RISC chips in 1992, it could draw on capabilities developed in its $6 billion semiconductor business. The two small firms, lacking their own semiconductor production facilities, used alliances to "match" the capabilities of the two large firms. (This is a rough measure of relevant capabilities, as not all semiconductor capacity is applicable to the RISC field. Even so, Mips designed its chip so that it could be produced on semiconductor lines intended for S-RAM chips, in an effort to benefit directly from its partners' capacity in S-RAMs.)

In the systems portion of the business, too, Mips and Sun used their alliances to approximate the scale of operations of the much-larger HP and IBM businesses. Because of Sun's early dominance of the technical workstation business, the Sun group sold more RISC workstations in 1992 than did any of the other groups ($3 billion). Considering that Mips had no head start in workstations, the $2.1 billion sales of its group is remarkable. The Mips sales figure is due to the strong collection of firms in this group, which included DEC and major Japanese and European firms. HP and IBM were not far behind Mips, but they relied mostly on their in-house capabilities.

Taking total microcomputer revenues as the measure of scale, the IBM group surpassed all the others because it combined the systems business of IBM and Apple. An alliance between two, or a few, large firms can thus overwhelm groups of smaller firms in terms of scale of operations. Still, the number of firms in a group remains important, regardless of their combined scale. IBM recognized this when it began in 1994 to distribute technical information to all firms, large or small, that were interested in making personal computers based on the PowerPC RISC chip.

In sum, the situation facing Mips and Sun was radically different than that facing the dominant niche firms discussed earlier. The niche players could rely on their in-house capabilities to battle their relatively smaller rivals. Small firms facing large rivals in a market with increasing returns to scale, on the other hand, cannot expect to succeed on their own—alliances are critical in expanding their reach. As they gather allies, these firms are transformed, or rather, they become part of a larger whole. The larger whole—the constellation—then competes against other firms and other sets of allies.

These results are consistent with studies of *Fortune 500* firms, which have found that dominant firms rarely use alliances (Gomes-Casseres 1996). As a general matter, alliance use is much more common among second- and third-tier players than among industry leaders. IBM, for example, has traditionally dominated the computer mainframe field and has almost no alliances in that business. But IBM has struggled in the personal computer field, where Intel and Microsoft dominate; in that business IBM has used alliances extensively, including its famous PowerPC alliance with Motorola and Apple. In other words, just as "small" firms can be "large" within their niche, so can "large" firms be "small" in comparison with their rivals. The logic of collaboration among *Fortune 500* firms is completely parallel to what was previously described—the relatively large firms shun alliances, while the relatively small firms use them to overcome disadvantages of scale.

## Competitive Advantage in Groups

When small firms create constellations of allies, what determines their competitive advantages? I propose to examine that question here with a simple conceptual framework. The appendix contains a more formal statement of this framework.

All firms—large and small—engaged in group-based competition can draw on two sources of competitive advantage. The first is group-based advantage; it is derived from who is in the group and how the group is managed. Competing groups are usually driven by the same underlying economic factors, such as economies of scale and scope. But precisely how the groups respond to these factors differentiates one from the other. This differentiation, in turn, can become a source of potential advantage or disadvantage.

The second source of advantage available to firms engaged in group-based competition is firm-based; it is derived from the distinctive capabilities of each firm. This conventional type of advantage takes on a special role in group-based competition. First, the pooling of these distinctive capabilities of firms in a group helps to create group-based advantages; there is thus a spillover effect whereby members of the group benefit from each other's firm-based advantages. Second, firm-based advantages determine the position and power of each firm within its group.

The benefits that each firm derives from participation in a group, therefore, are a function of the total benefits of the group and the firm's share of this total. This will be true of large as well as small firms. But in the case of small firms, their dependence on the group is likely to be greater than for larger firms, and so their share of the total will be correspondingly smaller.

## Total Benefits of the Group

The economic viability of a group depends on the existence of a positive "network effect"—this is the payoff to collaboration (Church and Gandal 1992). If the network effects were negative—that is, if an alliance between firms led to a *reduction* of their overall advantage—then there would not be any group surplus to distribute among members, and so no incentive for firms to stay together. With a positive network effect, the surplus created through collaboration is distributed among members.

The extent of the group-based advantages of a constellation depends on the design of the group. Alliances, as previously noted, are specific systems for controlling a set of capabilities. Therefore, the choice of which capabilities are in the group is one critical design decision; the second is how the control system is structured, because that determines whether the potential synergies among the capabilities are realized.

## The Share of Each Member

The share of the group surplus that each firm receives also depends on the design of the group, but in a different way. The network effect of a group is generated by the way the group's structure differentiates it from other groups and from single firms. This effect is attributable to the group as a whole and is identical for all members of the group, regardless of their position in the group. But the share that each member in fact receives from the group's surplus depends on the unique position of that member in relation to others in the network.

The total set of capabilities is not important in determining the share of each member, only the firm's capabilities *relative* to those of its partners. Firms can be thought of as bargaining over the spoils of their joint action; their contribution to the joint enterprise is then a prime source of bargaining power. We would expect that a firm contributing a highly valued capability is able to claim a higher share of the group surplus than one contributing something of lesser value. Furthermore, a firm may improve its bargaining power in the group by changing its position in the group.

## Benefits from Group Membership

The combination of network effects and network position is a distinguishing mark of collective competition. The competitive advantage of each member depends critically on who its partners are and on the structure of the alliances among the partners.

The benefits due to each member in a group vary with total network effects as well as with the bargaining power of each firm. As a result, it may appear attractive for a firm to join a group even if the network effects are low, as long as the firm can be enticed by a large share of total benefits. Conversely, a firm in a poor bargaining position may benefit little from participating in a powerful group, even when the total benefits of the network are high.

Network effects and bargaining power of members are likely to change over time as groups grow and relationships between members evolve. Because of these changes, firms may choose to join constellations even in the absence of immediate benefits if they expect network effects to rise with the growth of the group. Similarly, a member's position in a group may become more or less attractive over time, depending on its relative position. Ironically, the position of some firms may deteriorate as a group grows—their internal bargaining power may decline even while the overall economic power of the group increases.

## Risks of Constellations

The evidence suggests that Mips was substantially aided by its alliance group—it simply would not have survived beyond its infancy were it not for the alliance strategy and the support of Kubota, DEC, NEC, and other giants. Furthermore, its technology would not be in contention today were it not for ACE and the Mips alliance with Microsoft. But the fact that Mips ultimately merged with one of its partners (Silicon Graphics) demonstrates that alliance groups are not all-powerful; at the heart of the group there must be a viable firm. And, in fact, alliance strategies such as that of Mips carry high risks for the firm.

### *Loss of Control*

The extensive use of alliances leads to two problems of particular urgency for small firms: loss of control and loss of appropriability. Central to any alliance is a sharing of control (Stopford and Wells 1972). Even minority partners in a joint venture influence the decisions of the joint venture and thereby affect the degree of control of the majority partner. Licensers often allow others to use their technology in ways that may not be specified precisely in advance, and they usually have little control over the marketing of the end product. The more alliances a firm has, therefore, the more influence its partners will have on its destiny and overall performance. Firms that pursue business strategies centering around alliances—such as IBM in PCs, and Mips and Sun in RISC—run the risk of losing effective control over the performance of these businesses.

This loss of control manifests itself in various ways. One problem is that alliance groups may reduce the range of instruments available to the firm in implementing its business strategy. For example, a firm selling exclusively through Original Equipment Manufacturer (OEM) alliances usually lacks the ability to promote sales with advertising or direct sales forces. Mips also encountered problems with dependence on external suppliers, which in turn delayed the launch of critical new products.

Another way in which small firms risk losing control over their destiny as their alliance network grows is by a subtle shift in the center of gravity of the group. Initially, the loss of control is limited to bilateral alliances—a risk of technology leakage here, a loose marketing approach there. But, particularly for small firms building large groups, the network may begin to assume a life of its own. Mips began building its group consciously and carefully, and initially it had great success with this strategy. However, as its partners came to include giants such as Compaq, Microsoft, DEC, NEC, and Siemens, it became unclear who was in control. Particularly after ACE was formed, the strategy seemed to be succeeding and spinning out of control at the same time. From then on, Mips's future depended on ACE, and ACE, in turn, depended on collaboration among a handful of big players. In the end, a series of defections by Compaq, DEC, and others doomed both ACE and Mips.

*Limited Appropriability*

Besides forcing a sharing of control, alliances inevitably imply a sharing of returns. In equity joint ventures, profits are usually shared according to ownership percentages. Nonequity alliances also imply a sharing of profits, although the distribution among partners is less clear. Still, license contracts, for example, are notoriously poor at maximizing the return to the technology provider, due to high transaction costs. As a result, firms that rely heavily on licensing can expect to earn lower returns than comparable firms that are able to use their technology in their own operations (Caves, Crookell, and Killing 1983).

This appropriability problem is exacerbated when alliances are motivated by a race to diffuse the technology in a standards battle. The objective of technology diffusion contradicts the objective of profit maximization, at least in the short run—the fastest way to diffuse technology is to give it out freely. In reality, few firms go to this extreme, if only because they need to recoup costs of technology development and transfer. Still, firms that pursue alliance strategies with the objective of diffusing technology may suffer sluggish profitability early on. They may, of course, reap benefits in the long run, but only if over time they can increase their share of profits from their technology.

When a small firm expands its alliance group to promote its technology, it must thus cleverly maneuver a dangerous path. On the one hand, a large group usually helps spread its technology more quickly and widely. On the other hand, if the firm does not appropriate enough of the returns on its efforts, then it will lack the cash needed to invest in further R&D, causing it to fall behind competing technologies.

That is what happened to Mips. Without sufficient profits to invest, Mips could not maintain product leadership. At the same time, rivals HP, IBM, and Intel redoubled their investments and R&D efforts. A powerful new generation of Mips chips arrived too late to counter this onslaught. The growth of an alliance group in a competitive standards game thus may represent either a virtuous or a vicious cycle, depending on how growth is managed, and, possibly, contained (Conner 1992).

## Conclusion

This essay has shown that there is no such thing as the typical small firm, at least not as regards their alliance and general business strategies. It may well be that all firms of a certain size share certain characteristics, such as flat organizational structures or nimbleness. But we have seen how these firms can follow one of two different approaches to alliances, depending on their *relative size.* Firms that are small relative to competitors and to the requirements of the market tend to use alliances to reach scale and scope; firms that are large relative to the same benchmarks rely on internal capabilities. Both types of firms, it should be noted, use alliances according to the same logic. Their starting conditions—not the costs and benefits of alliances—are what differs.

This essay did not attempt to test formal hypotheses, but rather to generate arguments and concepts useful in further research. The analysis suggests two general hypotheses to be addressed in future work:

1. *The importance of alliances in the strategy of a small firm will rise with the importance of scale economies in its market and decline with the size of the firm relative to its competitors.* In other words, small firms will seek scale through alliances if that is required for competitive success in their market; but they are less likely to do so if they occupy a niche in which they themselves are large relative to competitors.

2. *The benefits that a small firm can derive from a constellation will rise with the sum of the capabilities assembled in the constellation as well as*

*with the capabilities of the firm relative to its partners in the constellation.* More broadly, small firms will benefit from the total value created in their network; but their share of these benefits will depend on their bargaining power within the network. The net gains to the firm depend on the interaction between these two factors. The concepts of "total value" and "bargaining power" can, of course, be operationalized in different ways; the various measures of capability used here are examples only.

There is a more general conclusion and perhaps a paradox in the arguments and stylized evidence considered in this essay. We saw that there are two types of small firms in terms of the propensity to use alliances. Both types of firms, it appears, succeed because the firms find ways to *overcome their smallness.* The deep-niche firms do so by finding markets in which there are no large rivals, that is, markets in which they can act as large players. The other firms—which do have large rivals—seek allies to nullify their disadvantages; the new unit of competition that is created in that way transcends the small firm itself.

Why do small firms need to overcome their smallness? The pervasiveness of scale economies in modern industry is probably the chief reason. Very few modern industries can be said to have no scale economies in any part of their value chain. And deregulation and globalization in the 1980s and early 1990s have only served to reduce the number of markets in which subscale firms can survive.

Yet, the venture capital business is booming, even in industries with demonstrated economies of scale, such as computers. One reason may be that emerging businesses are tailor-made for small firms; they often require flexibility, personal creativity, business focus, and commitment—all characteristics that we generally associate with small firms. Even so, more and more new ventures seem to require alliances for legitimacy or for reaching minimum scale and scope in key parts of the value chain. Furthermore, returns to scale are likely to increase as the new businesses mature, leading to a new demand for alliances.

## APPENDIX: THE PROFITS OF FIRMS IN GROUPS: A SIMPLE MODEL

This appendix presents a limited formal model of the determinants of profitability of firms competing in groups. It does not attempt to explain why firms choose to form groups or how many groups can exist in an industry. Rather, it identifies the sources of value (or profit) that become available to a firm, given that it has decided to participate in a group.

The profits that firm $i$ derives from participation in group $G$ can be defined as follows:

$$\pi_i^G = \pi^G \, . \, \alpha_i \tag{1}$$

where

$\pi^G$ = total profits of group $G$
$\alpha_i$ = the share of firm $i$ in group $G$'s profits.

The total profits of group $G$ are the sum of the profits that group members would have generated in the absence of the group, multiplied by a factor $\sigma$ that represents the "synergy" or "network effect" of the group:

$$\pi^G = \pi_n \, . \, \sigma \tag{2}$$

where

$\pi_n$ = sum of the profits of the $n$ firms in the group, in the absence of the group
$\sigma > 0$.

The share of firm $i$ in group $G$'s profits can be assumed to be based on the ratio of the profits that the members would have had without the group, multiplied by a factor $r_i$ representing the "extra" bargaining power of firm $i$ in the group:

$$\alpha_i = \pi_i / \pi_n \, . \, \rho_i \tag{3}$$

where

$\pi_i$ = profits of firm $i$ in the absence of the group
$\rho_i > 0$; and
$\Sigma \, \alpha_i = 1$.

Substituting (3) and (2) into (1) gives:

$$\pi_i^G = \pi_i \, . \, \sigma \, . \, \rho_i. \tag{4}$$

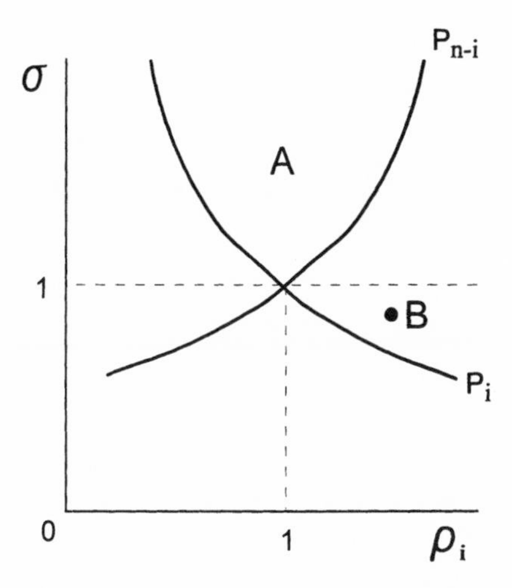


**Fig. 3. Profits of firms in groups**

Equation (4) can be interpreted to mean that the profits a firm derives from participating in a group depend on three factors:

1. Its own firm-specific advantages, which are its sole source of profits if the group has no network effect ($\sigma = 1$) and if the firm has no bargaining power to increase its return in the group ($\rho_i = 1$);

2. The network effect generated by the group's organization (but not the firm-specific advantages of the other group members); and

3. The firm's bargaining power based on its position in the group (again, claims based purely on relative firm-specific advantages are not important).

These conclusions help delineate certain regions in the mapping of $\sigma$ against $\rho_i$ (fig. 3).

The figure shows the iso-profit lines for Firm $i$ ($P_i$) and for the rest of the group's members collectively ($P_{n-i}$). Both curves are drawn to go through the point 1,1, where profits from group participation are equal to profits without the group.

The figure illustrates the necessary conditions for the sustainability of a group. In the region to the upper right of $P_i$, Firm $i$ is better off with the group than without it. In the region to the upper left of $P_{n-i}$, Firms $n - i$ are better off with the group than without it. These two regions overlap in region A, which is the only region where all firms are better off. In all other regions, cooperation will not be sustainable, because one firm or another, or all, will be worse off inside than outside the group.

The figure also helps illustrate when a firm might join groups whose organization fails to add to the total profits of the members ($\sigma < 1$). Any given firm might be willing to do this if it can acquire a sufficiently large claim on the group's profits, that is, if it can exploit the other group members ($\rho_i > 1$). For example, Firm $i$ would be willing to join at point B.

But the other members (Firms $n-i$) would not be willing to join at point B, because it is to the bottom right of $P_{n-i}$—they are better off staying out of the group. However, they might be willing to join if they expected that the network effects were increasing with time or with group size, so that A would move upward and into the shaded region. Bandwagon growth can arise when this expectation is based on group size.

## REFERENCES

Acs, Zoltan J., et al. 1999. "The Internationalization of Small and Medium-Sized Enterprises." In this volume.

Buckley, Peter J., et al. 1983. *Direct Investment in the United Kingdom by Smaller European Firms.* London: Macmillan.

Buckley, Peter J., and Hafiz Mirza. 1997. "The Role of Small and Medium Sized Enterprises in Technology Transfer to Less Developed Countries—In the Case of the U.K." In *International Technology Transfer by Small and Medium Sized Enterprises: Country Studies,* ed. Peter J. Buckley et al., 243–99. New York: St. Martin's Press.

Caves, Richard E. 1982. *Multinational Enterprise and Economic Analysis.* Cambridge: Cambridge University Press.

Caves, Richard E., Harold Crookell, and J. Peter Killing. 1983. "The Imperfect Market for Technology Licenses." *Oxford Bulletin of Economics and Statistics* 45 (3): 249–67.

Chandler, Alfred D., Jr. 1990. "The Enduring Logic of Industrial Success." *Harvard Business Review* (Mar.–Apr.): 130–40.

Church, Jeffrey, and Neil Gandal. 1992. "Network Effects, Software Provision, and Standardization." *Journal of Industrial Economics* (Mar.): 85–103.

Conner, Kathleen. 1992. "Obtaining Strategic Advantage from Being Imitated: When Can Encouraging 'Clones' Pay?" Sept., mimeographed.

Cusumano, Michael, Yiorgos Mylonadis, and Richard S. Rosenbloom. 1992. "Strategic Maneuvering and Mass-Market Dynamics: The Triumph of VHS over Beta." *Business History Review* (spring): 51–94.

Gomes-Casseres, Benjamin. 1988. "Joint Venture Cycles: The Evolution of Ownership Strategies of U.S. MNEs: 1945–1975." In *Cooperative Strategies in International Business,* ed. Farok Contractor and Peter Lorange, 111–28. Lexington, MA: Lexington Books.

———. 1994. "Group versus Group: How Alliance Networks Compete." *Harvard Business Review* (July–Aug.): 62+.

———. 1996. *The Alliance Revolution: The New Shape of Business Rivalry.* Cambridge, MA: Harvard University Press.

Gomes-Casseres, Benjamin, and Tomás Kohn. 1997. "Small Firms in International Competition: A Challenge to Traditional Theory?" In *International Technology Transfer by Small and Medium Sized Enterprises: Country Studies,* ed. Peter J. Buckley et al., 280–96. New York: St. Martin's Press.

Hackett, Donald W. 1977. "Penetrating International Markets: Key Considerations for Smaller Firms." *Journal of Small Business Management* (Jan.): 10–16.

Horst, Thomas. 1972. "Firm and Industry Determinants of the Decision of Invest Abroad: An Empirical Study." *Review of Economics and Statistics* (Aug.): 258–66.

Kohn, Tomás O. 1988. "International Entrepreneurship: Foreign Direct Investment by Small U.S.-Based Manufacturing Firms." D.B.A. diss., Harvard University.

Mascarenhas, Briance. 1986. "International Strategies of Non-Dominant Firms." *Journal of International Business Studies* (spring): 1–25.

Namiki, Nobuaki. 1988. "Export Strategy for Small Business." *Journal of Small Business Management* (Apr.): 32–37.

Newbould, Gerald D., et al. 1978. *Going International: The Experience of Smaller Companies Overseas.* New York: John Wiley and Sons.

Niosi, Jorge. 1997. "Canadian Technology Transfer to Developing Countries by Small and Medium Enterprises." In *International Technology Transfer by Small and Medium Sized Enterprises: Country Studies,* ed. Peter J. Buckley et al., 87–112. New York: St. Martin's Press.

Ozawa, Terutomo. 1997. "Technology Transfers by Japan's Small and Medium Enterprises." In *International Technology Transfer by Small and Medium Sized Enterprises: Country Studies,* ed. Peter J. Buckley et al., 212–42. New York: St. Martin's Press.

Penrose, Edith T. 1980. *The Theory of the Growth of the Firm.* White Plains: M. E. Sharpe. (Originally published by Basil Blackwell, 1959.)

Stopford, John, and Louis T. Wells, Jr. 1972. *Managing the Multinational Enterprise.* New York: Basic Books.

Sweeney, James K. 1970. "A Small Company Enters the European Market." *Harvard Business Review* (Sept.–Oct.): 126–32.

U.S. Department of Commerce. 1992. *U.S. Direct Investment Abroad: 1989 Benchmark Survey Data.* Washington, DC: Government Printing Office.

Vernon, Raymond. 1970. "Organization as a Scale Factor in the Growth of Firms." In *Industrial Organization and Economic Development,* ed. Jesse W. Markham and Gustav F. Papanek, 47–66. Boston: Houghton Mifflin.

Vlachoutsikos, Charalambos. 1989. "How Small- to Mid-Sized U.S. Firms Can Profit from *Perestroika.*" *California Management Review* (spring): 91–112.

# Small Firms as International Players

*Tomás O. Kohn*

As Gomes-Casseres points out in the introduction to his "Alliance Strategies of Small Firms" essay (this volume): "Students of international business have traditionally believed that success in foreign markets required large size." Given this traditional view, if a firm is not large yet wishes to compete globally, it has two less-than-pleasant options: the first one, give up on its dreams and stay frustrated in its domestic market; the second one, give up on its independence and seek help from other, larger, players. If these were the only options, managers of small firms in "global" industries would be either myopic (those not interested in the international arena), frustrated (those who wish to go abroad, but can't), or good team players—not independent leaders (those who seek others' help). Yet as one looks at the ranks of small-firm managers, one could hardly characterize them this way. Something must be wrong with the analysis; the question is what? Does the problem rest in the "traditional" assumption, crisply stated by Chandler, that "to compete globally you have to be big," (1990) or does it rest in the way I have characterized small-firm managers?

The work Gomes-Casseres and I did (1997), based on a limited sample of small firms with international affiliates, suggested that the problem may rest on the "traditional" assumption. After all, 92 percent of the foreign ventures in our sample were majority-owned. The sample, however, was very small. While it allowed us to explore these firms' activities in depth, it did not enable us to generalize further. In this essay I will report on a study of all U.S. foreign-investing firms that reported their activities in the U.S. Department of Commerce's 1982 Benchmark Survey (1992) to see if the findings may be further generalized.

## International Activities of Small Firms

Evidence shows that small firms are, against the expectations of many traditional scholars, active players in the international arena. As can be seen in table 1, small and medium-sized parent firms represented almost 50 percent of all U.S. foreign-investing firms in 1982. I prepared table 1 based on U.S. manufacturing firms' foreign investment behavior as reported by the Commerce Department's U.S. Direct Investment Abroad: 1982 Benchmark Survey (1985). I divided all U.S. foreign-investing firms (parents) into four size categories, based on their employment in the United States (10–499 = small; 500–1,999 = medium; 2,000–9,999 = large; >9,999 = very large). The 1,215 manufacturing parents and their 11,231 manufacturing affiliates are the sample on which the data presented in this essay are based. The methods and data used are described in detail in Kohn 1988.

## Affiliate Ownership Practices

Clearly, many small firms are able to invest abroad. That being the case, one must establish what it is that enables these firms to operate where so many doubt that they may tread. The first answer that comes to mind is that they tread abroad when they are aided by others. Do the data support this answer? Surprisingly, no! I found that the tendency of small foreign-investing firms to form affiliates that are minority-, as opposed to majority-, owned is actually lower than the tendency of large parents to do so. That being the case, those small firms that invest internationally must be able to go abroad with little help from others. But how?

One may argue that the answer to this apparent anomaly lies in the type of activities small firms are engaged in when they venture abroad. Some parent firms may be involved abroad in a wide range of activities, going from research and development, to manufacturing and, finally, to marketing. Such activities would require substantial financial and managerial resources and would, in the classical view, be off-limits to small firms without others' help. Other parent firms may be involved abroad only in marketing activities, and that would—at least in the case of producer goods where the task of adapting products to host-country consumer tastes is minimized—require relatively few resources. Given these arguments, one would expect—with traditional reasoning—that the observed ownership pattern could be explained if most small-firm foreign affiliates were devoted to marketing

**Table 1. Size Distribution of U.S. Foreign Direct Investors, 1982 (number of manufacturing parents and manufacturing affiliates)**

| | Parent Size Category | | | | |
|---|---|---|---|---|---|
| | Small | Medium | Large | Very Large | Total |
| Parents | 214 | 382 | 372 | 247 | 1,215 |
| Affiliates | 331 | 1,038 | 2,672 | 7,190 | 11,231 |

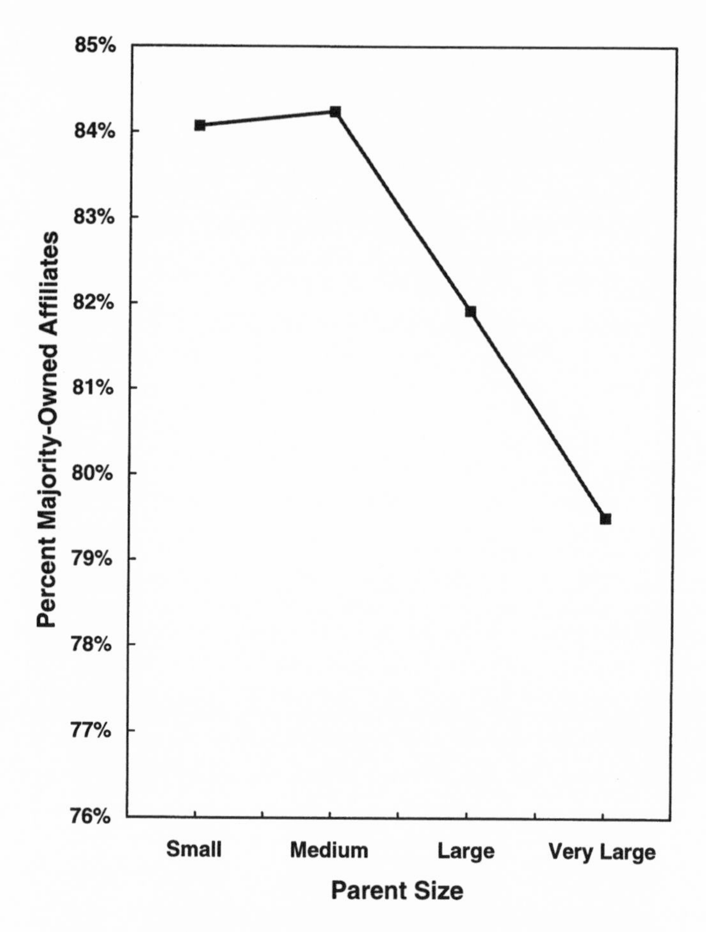


**Fig. 1. Affiliate ownership: All manufacturing affiliates**

and not to manufacturing activities. To eliminate this possible explanation, I concentrated my analysis on the ownership pattern of different-sized parent firms' manufacturing affiliates. I found again the same tendency of smaller firms to have fewer minority-owned affiliates than large firms (fig. 1).

Another possible explanation of the observed data could be that smaller U.S. foreign-investing firms tend to locate most of their affiliates in Canada, a place where the costs of doing business abroad are minimized, while larger firms operate in environments that are more diverse, and hence more costly to do business in. To test this line of reasoning I looked at the ownership pattern of manufacturing affiliates in Canada. Once again the pattern (fig. 2) was repeated: smaller firms tend to have fewer minority-owned affiliates than larger firms.

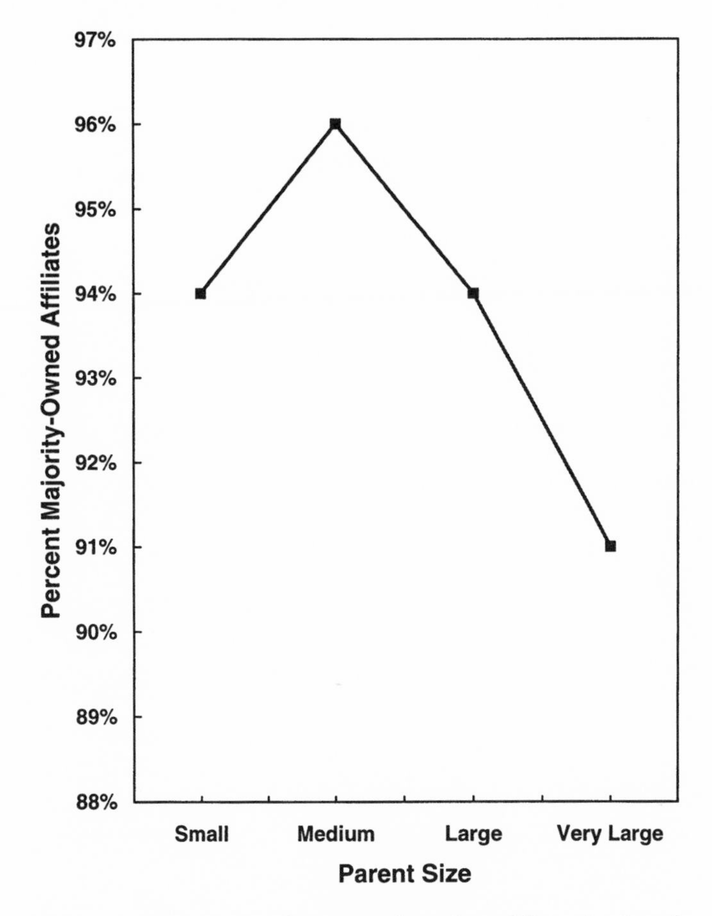


**Fig. 2. Affiliate ownership: Manufacturing affiliates in Canada**

To further explore the possibility that affiliate location may be a driver of affiliate ownership by small firms, I repeated the test for manufacturing affiliates located in Japan, where the arguments about the cost of doing business for U.S. firms would essentially be the opposite of those for Canada. Again, the same pattern was evident (fig. 3).

It seems that the affiliate-ownership practices of the few firms Gomes-Casseres and I studied are representative of the population of small U.S. firms that reported their international investments in the 1982 Benchmark Survey.

The consistency of the patterns one observes in the preceding figures effectively lays to rest the idea that small firms are able to invest abroad because they compensate for their lack of size by seeking, more so than large firms, partners for their international activities. If this idea is laid to rest,

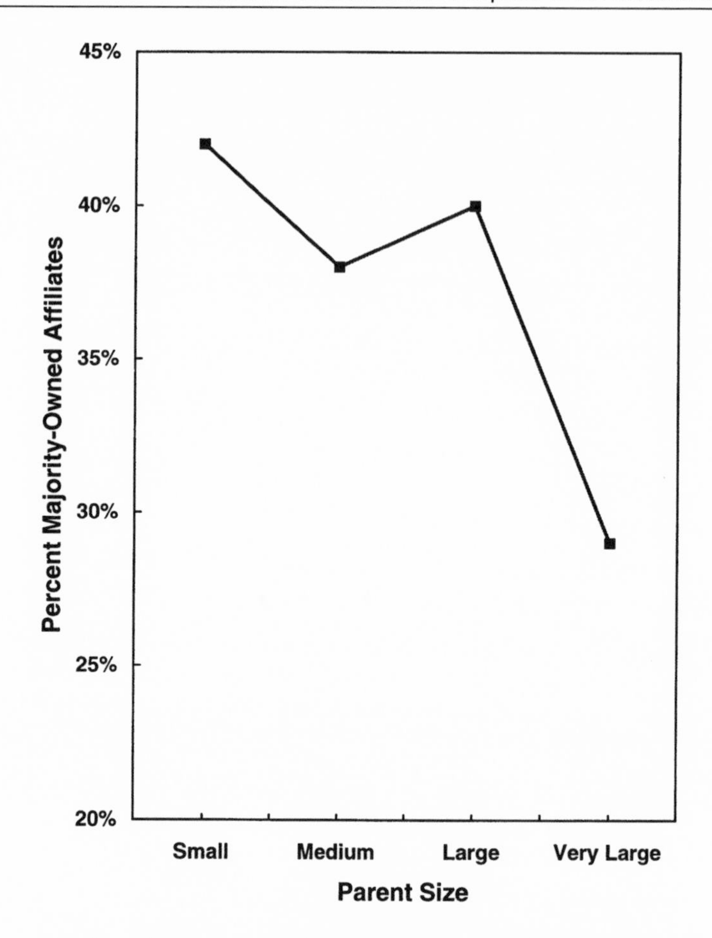


**Fig. 3. Affiliate ownership: Manufacturing affiliates in Japan**

then so must the argument behind it, namely, that affiliate ownership policies are driven by these firms' difficulties in covering the costs of doing business abroad. Given that, in fact, these difficulties are likely to be great, one must ask what arguments may explain the observed patterns? I argue that one way to explain the patterns is to explore these firms' strategies.

## Firm Strategy

Gomes-Casseres and I found that the firms we studied followed what we call a "deep niche" strategy. These firms' behavior was characterized by positions of market dominance and technological leadership, and by a focus on producer goods. I will explore these findings using, once again, the aggregate data of the Benchmark Survey.

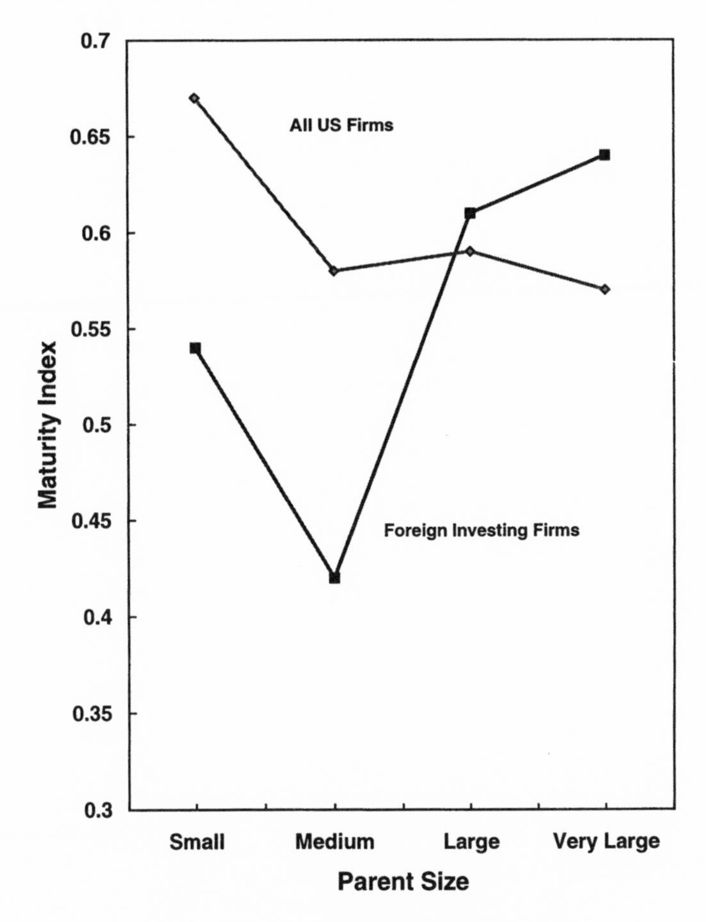


**Fig. 4. Maturity: Industry maturity index**

## Market Dominance

One would expect that the industries in which a small firm can be a dominant player are limited. Specifically, one may surmise that in emerging industries, before the consolidation that tends to occur in more mature industries has taken place, firms do not have to be very large to be dominant players. That being the case, one would expect that if small foreign-investing firms are dominant players in their industries they will tend to be concentrated in emerging industries.

To test this hypothesis, I constructed an industry-maturity index and plotted the weighted average maturity of different size firms' industries against firm size. I did so for all manufacturing firms in the United States and also for those firms that have direct investments abroad. The results are shown in figure 4.

The pattern one expects if these small firms are dominant players is present: small, and even more so medium-sized, foreign-investing firms come from the least mature industries. It is in these emerging industries that small firms can be active international players. As Gomes-Casseres suggests, these firms may be small in absolute terms, but probably large within their industries. Being, therefore, industry leaders, these firms resist sharing affiliate ownership; something others have found (Stopford and Wells 1972; Gomes-Casseres 1985) in their ownership strategies studies.

One can learn more about the characteristics of small foreign-investing firms if one analyzes the differences between the industries from which foreign-investing and all U.S. firms originate. One observes that while small and medium-sized foreign-investing firms originate in industries whose maturity index is substantially lower than the index for their domestic counterparts, the opposite is true for large and very large firms. One can understand these differences by exploring the strategic motivations that lead firms to invest abroad.

For large and very large firms, these motivations have been explained at length by proponents of the product cycle theories of foreign direct investment (Vernon 1966, 1979; Wells 1972; Stopford and Wells 1972; Davidson 1980; Knickerbocker 1973; and others). In this model, foreign direct investment is mostly a defensive move to protect the firm against loss of export markets and against competition from low-cost foreign producers, producers that spring up once the technological advantages of the firm are eroded. Such defensive moves are likely to be a major factor in relatively mature industries where technology has become widespread and standardized.

For smaller firms, the motivations that lead to foreign investment are likely to be quite different. Small firms operating in emerging industries face unique threats and opportunities. The threats revolve around the frailty of the technological leadership they may possess. Such leadership is frail because of the risk that their technology will be copied or that new developments may make the technology obsolete. The opportunities revolve around the possibility of gaining first-mover advantages that will give them the desired leadership position in the as-yet-unstructured industry. Gaining such advantages abroad is particularly important for a small, highly focused firm. It must preempt, as far as possible, the emergence of competitors within its narrow area of expertise. Given the technological parity between many developed countries, competitors are likely to emerge both at home and abroad.

Still, the desire to gain first-mover advantages is likely to be only one of several forces that may motivate the small firm in emerging industries to invest abroad. Maybe more important is the contribution that a manufacturing affiliate abroad may make to the firm's sources of competitive advantage. As has been pointed out (Schmookler 1966, and others), innovations are the result of the interplay between the firm and its environment. In view of this, a firm operating in various environments will be more likely to generate a variety of innovations related to its core technology than a firm operating only in its home country. For a small firm, with all its eggs in one basket, remaining at the forefront of its narrow technological niche is vital. Such a firm can ill afford to miss out on the innovations that may result from the interplay between its activities with different environments. The same argument does not apply to larger firms. Since they are likely to have their eggs in many baskets, their competitive advantages are not so vulnerable to innovations elsewhere, and, therefore, they are not so singularly driven to invest abroad so as to stay alive.

These arguments suggest that investing abroad represents a valuable move for a small firm in an emerging industry, an option that may, when incorporated into the firm's strategy, result in the market dominance that Gomes-Casseres and I observed in our limited sample.

## Focus on Producer Goods

To find out if, on average, small foreign-investing firms tend to focus on producer goods, I constructed a "consumer intensity" index and plotted the weighted average consumer intensity of different size firms' industries against firm size (fig. 5). The index provides a measure of the extent to which products from a given industry are sold directly to consumers and allows me to refine on the dichotomous world of consumer and producer goods. Once again, I did so for all manufacturing firms in the United States and for firms with direct investments abroad.

Clearly, the aggregate data support the small-sample results Gomes-Casseres and I observed: small foreign-investing firms tend to concentrate in producer goods. Given the observed pattern, the question arises: why should small firms that invest abroad concentrate in low consumer intensity industries while those that operate in the United States do not? The answer may lie in small firms' ability, or lack thereof, to deal with the costs of modifying their products when they sell them abroad. It is reasonable to state that the higher an industry's consumer intensity, the more likely it is that the industry's output needs to be modified to conform with host-country tastes and marketing methods. Domestically, on the other hand, product and marketing adaptation are not an issue. Therefore, within the United States there is no reason to expect differences between small and large firms' tendency to operate in either high or low consumer intensity industries.

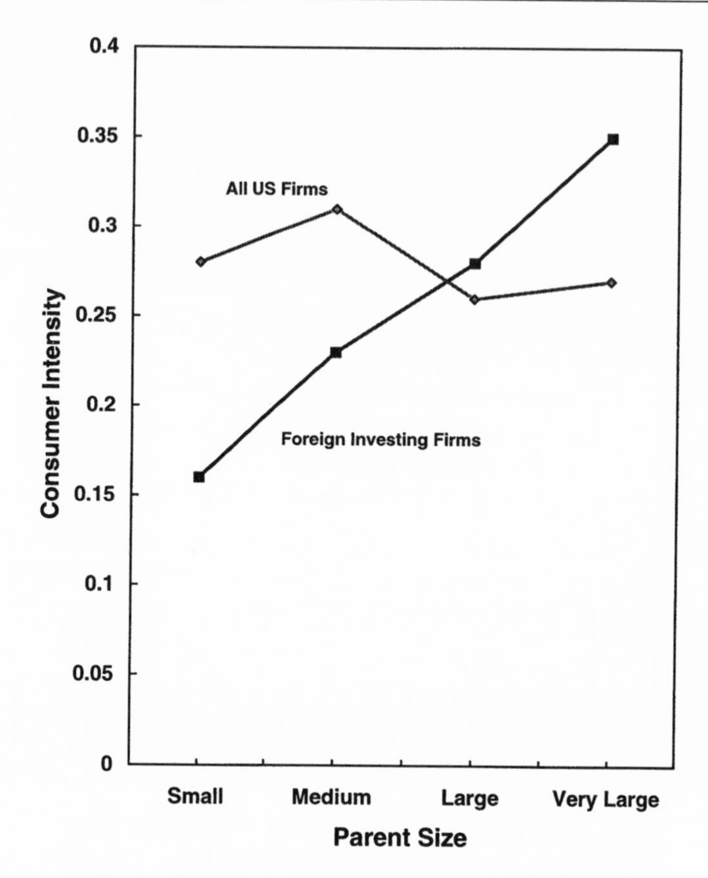


**Fig. 5. Consumer intensity: Consumer intensity index**

In foreign environments, however, the situation is quite different. Only large firms are able to absorb the costs of making the product and marketing modifications necessary in high consumer intensity industries. Given their lack of resources, small firms—unable to bear the adaptation costs mentioned earlier—will be limited to low consumer intensity industries.

## Technological Leadership

Yet, even if small firms avoid the high costs of adapting products and marketing methods when they invest abroad, one must still inquire into what advantages, if any, these small firms have over their host-country competitors. As has been argued extensively (Buckley and Casson 1976; Caves 1982; Hennart 1980; Stopford and Wells 1972; Vernon 1966; and others), such advantages are necessary to compensate for the costs of doing business

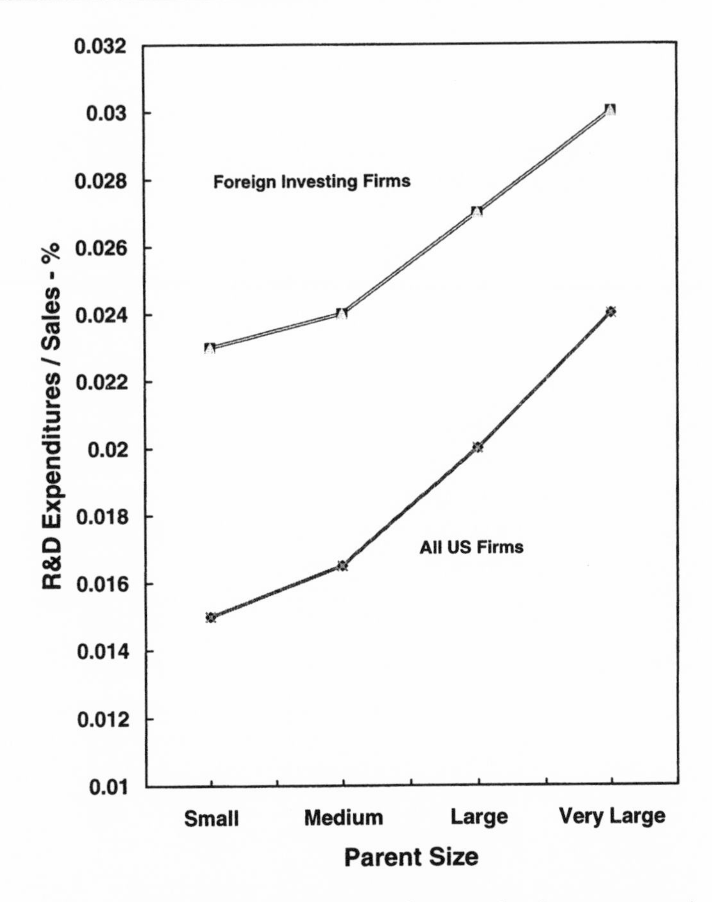


**Fig. 6. R&D intensity: R&D expenditures/sales (in percentages)**

abroad. Companies that are the technological leaders in their industries would, certainly, have the necessary advantages to compete internationally. Therefore, it was not surprising when Gomes-Casseres and I found that the firms in our small sample fit this description.

At an aggregate level, therefore, one would expect to see that most small firms investing abroad rely on R&D-based technological advantages. (They are not likely to rely on advertising-based advantages because these would have to be adapted to host country environments, and that would be costly.) Large firms, on the other hand, may rely on either advertising- or R&D-based advantages in their international operations.

While the aggregate data of the Benchmark Survey do not lend themselves to a direct test of this idea, they do provide some insights. As can be seen in figure 6, a comparison of the R&D intensity of the industries in which small foreign-investing firms operate shows that these firms come from industries whose R&D intensity is much greater than the R&D intensity of the industries in which small firms operate domestically. Additionally, the difference in R&D intensity between small and large foreign-investing firms' industries is less than the equivalent difference among firms operating domestically. These facts lend support to the idea that, in general, small firms that compete abroad are able to do so because of their technological capabilities.

## Conclusion

In his analysis, "Alliance Strategies of Small Firms," Gomes-Casseres identified what appears to be a bimodal distribution in the propensity of small firms to collaborate with others. Among small firms, one group's propensity to collaborate with others is higher than average while another's is lower than average. Regarding both groups of firms, Gomes-Casseres bases his findings on a limited number of observations. Are these anomalies, or do they really represent a broader population of small firms? In this essay I have shown that, based on an analysis of aggregate data, we can confidently state that there are large numbers of small firms that, in fact, "go it alone." I have also shown that their behavior is consistent with the "deep-niche" strategy Gomes-Casseres and I described as characteristic of these firms. These firms tend to be dominant players in their markets, to be technological leaders, and to operate mostly in producer goods industries. What I have not shown is whether the other group of small firms, those that are alliance-prone, also represents a broad population of firms. That issue remains to be answered.

Regarding the go-it-alone firms, Gomes-Casseres highlights the importance of these firms' ability to find markets where there are no large rivals so they may survive as "small" players. I would question whether such markets are, in fact, out there to be found. Maybe part of these firms' success rests on their ability, based on a combination of technological prowess and management skills, to create such markets. Large firms may, in practice, stay away from activities where capable small players are fully satisfying their customers' needs.

It would be interesting to apply Gomes-Casseres's context-capabilities-control framework to these go-it-alone firms to see if they may, in fact, be likely candidates for membership in alliance networks. One could argue that the context in which these firms operate—mostly producer goods industries—requires that they be the best suppliers their industrial customers can find. This requires two capabilities: (1) extreme levels of expertise and (2) close supplier–customer collaboration. By following the "deep-niche" strategy that characterizes the go-it-alone small firms they acquire the first of these capabilities. Therefore, at least in this regard, these firms need no alliances. However, how are these firms to acquire the second of these capabilities? I surmise that one way to do so is for these firms to structure alliances. These alliances, however, would be practically devoid of any equity participation and would rest more on long-term supply or other types of joint decision-making arrangements, somewhat akin to arrangements that exist within Japanese Sogo-soshas.

It may be interesting to point out that my analysis of small foreign-investing firms led me repeatedly to the conclusion that these firms must be endowed with the creative managerial practices often associated with entrepreneurial firms. The thoughts previously expressed bring up this topic again. It would be consistent with the management practices of entrepreneurs to follow what may appear to be two contradictory strategies at the same time: to insist on establishing wholly owned operations while at the same time structuring alliances. This makes sense if they shun others' help in those activities that are at the core of their sources of competitive advantage while they seek alliances in the rest of their activities. The kind of disaggregation of the value chain implicit in such behavior has been much talked about in recent management writings.

Finally, it is interesting to speculate on the motivation for alliance formation by these firms. On the one hand, it may be aimed at acquiring the capabilities they lack, following Gomes-Casseres's model. On the other hand, it may be designed as a defensive move to fend off backward-vertical integration by their large customers—customers who could easily become rivals or who would swallow them up if they were not totally satisfied with the products and services they receive from these small independent firms.

## REFERENCES

Buckley, Peter J., and Mark Casson. 1976. *The Future of the Multinational Enterprise.* London: Macmillan.

Caves, Richard E. 1982. *Multinational Enterprise and Economic Analysis.* Cambridge: Cambridge University Press.

Chandler, Alfred D. 1990. "The Enduring Logic of Industrial Success." *Harvard Business Review* (Mar.–Apr.): 130–40.

Davidson, William H. 1980. "The Location of Foreign Direct Investment Activity: Country Characteristics and Experience Effects." *Journal of International Business Studies* 11:9–22.

Gomes-Casseres, Benjamin. 1999. "Alliance Strategies of Small Firms." In this volume.

Gomes-Casseres, Benjamin, and Tomás O. Kohn. 1997. "Small Firms in International Competition: A Challenge to Traditional Theory?" In Peter J. Buckley et al., eds.,

*International Technology Transfer by Small and Medium Sized Enterprises: Country Studies,* 280–96. London: Macmillan.

Hennart, Jean-François. 1980. *A Theory of Multinational Enterprise.* Ann Arbor: University of Michigan Press.

Knickerbocker, F. T. 1973. *Oligopolistic Reaction and Multinational Enterprise.* Boston: Harvard University, Graduate School of Business Administration.

Kohn, Tomás O. 1988. "International Entrepreneurship: Foreign Direct Investment by Small U.S.–Based Manufacturing Firms." Doctoral diss., Harvard University, Graduate School of Business.

Schmookler, Jacob. 1966. *Invention and Economic Growth.* Cambridge, MA: Harvard University Press.

Stopford, John, and Louis T. Wells, Jr. 1972. *Managing the Multinational Enterprise: Organization of the Firm and Ownership of Subsidiaries.* New York: Basic Books.

U.S. Department of Commerce, Bureau of Economic Analysis. 1985. *U.S. Direct Investment Abroad: 1982 Benchmark Survey Data.* Washington, DC: U.S. Government Printing Office.

Vernon, Raymond. 1966. "International Investment and International Trade in the Product Cycle." *Quarterly Journal of Economics* 80:190–207.

———. 1979. "New Product Cycle Hypothesis in a New International Environment." *Oxford Bulletin of Economics and Statistics* 41 (4): 255–67.

Wells, Louis T., Jr., ed. 1972. *The Product Life Cycle and International Trade.* Boston: Division of Research, Graduate School of Business Administration, Harvard University.

PART 3

# Technological Diversity and Knowledge Spillovers

# The Exploration of Technological Diversity and Geographic Localization in Innovation

*Paul Almeida and Bruce Kogut*

Why should geographic space matter to the evident role played by small firms in exploring new technological opportunities? Despite the confusing array of findings regarding the relationship between size and innovation, the evidence is reasonably strong that small firms are more productive in the generation of innovations than larger firms. Though as an aggregate they spend considerably less on R&D, they produce new innovations with twice the productivity of larger firms (Acs and Audretsch 1990). Bound et al. (1984) similarly found higher rates of research productivity for smaller firms as measured by patents. However, these results are influenced by variations in technological opportunities among industries and in the national location. The higher productivity of small firm research is evident in only some industries and is more conclusive for the United States than for other countries (Scherer 1984; Pavitt, Robson, and Townsend 1987).

The findings on small firm innovations suggest a sea of change in our understanding of the perennial question of the relationship between firm size and innovation. The evidence, rather, points to the role played by the birth of start-ups in fields of high technological opportunity as an important driver of radical innovation. The lack of robustness of the relationship between firm size and innovation is not surprising in the light that size is a moving target driven, partly, by a firm's research success. Based on varying interpretations of Schumpeter's reflections on the routinization of research in the large laboratory, most studies have sought a cross-sectional relationship between firm size and innovation. But the cross-sectional evidence, as Cohen and Levin (1989) conclude in their review, is very mixed. There appears to be no hard and fast statement regarding optimal firm size or scale economies in reference to innovative activities.

The change in perspective, however, extends beyond seeing size and innovation as linked in a dynamic process. There is a broader way to understand the relationship, as first suggested by Jewkes, Sawers, and Stillerman. "It may well be," they note, "that there is no optimum size of firm but merely an optimal pattern for any industry, such as distribution of firms by size, character and outlook as to guarantee the most effective gathering together and commercially perfecting of the flow of new ideas" (1958, 168; cited in Cohen and Levin 1989, 1073–74). This line of inquiry presents the important questions why, in some industries and in some countries, small firms are more productive in the generation of new knowledge and how larger firms can be viable if they are inefficient. Cohen and Klepper (1996) propose that these two questions are linked. Small firms may be superior in the generation of new knowledge in industries characterized by technological opportunities. Larger firms are superior in their ability to appropriate returns from these innovations, either by buying and selling property rights (sometimes through cooperative ventures), acquiring the firms, or benefiting through spillovers.

If the focus is shifted from the optimal size of firms to "effective" size distributions, a puzzle concerns what sustains the viability of small firm innovative activity. In this essay, we argue that when small firms are understood as start-ups, they can be seen as playing two important roles in the exploration of technology and local networks. In many industries, start-ups receive funding because they explore new technological spaces and opportunities that are ignored by larger firms. Since their technological exploration is facilitated through close ties to other innovating institutions and start-up firms, their activities also, however, generate a geographic space in which knowledge of their research diffuses more rapidly within a local network of firms. As long as this technological space is sufficiently rich, the interaction of diffusion and innovation creates a positive feedback that reinforces further innovative efforts. This combination of the exploration of technological diversity and local firm networks contains the answer to two questions: why small firms in high technological opportunity industries are more productive in their research, and why innovative activity appears to have a spatial character.

We analyze the technological activity of small and large firms through the examination of patent data in the semiconductor industry. A statistical analysis of the technology classes in which small and large firms patent shows that while large firms dominate patenting in well-established areas, small (start-up) firms produce important innovations in smaller, less crowded fields. The examination of patent citation data indicates that start-ups are integrated into local knowledge networks to a greater degree than larger firms. Thus, we suggest there is a common explanation to why small firms are productive and the diffusion of innovations has a spatial character: the generation of new knowledge is facilitated by small firm networks.

## Technological Diversity and Start-up Networks

The conventional explanation for the role played by small firms in high innovation industries has appealed to the deficiency of internal incentives and flexibility in larger companies. (Monopolistic motivations are pertinent in industries less characterized by the potential for the introduction of radical innovations.) The attention paid to Schumpeter's discussion on the routinizing of innovation often neglects the other side of the equation, namely, his earlier emphasis on the dynamic role played by new firm innovations. His pessimism over the supply of entrepreneurs (1943, 152) led him to characterize the process of "creative destruction" as increasingly driven by large firms that are capable of innovating within a "routinized" regime.

There is substantial qualitative evidence supporting the role of small firms and individuals in introducing "radical" innovations. While examining fifty important and successful innovations introduced in this century, Jewkes, Sawers, and Stillerman (1958) found that a critical role was played by the individual inventor—more than half of these innovations were introduced outside established research organizations. Scherer and Ross (1990) highlight several "revolutionary" inventions by start-up firms that departed significantly from the technologies in use at the time of the invention. Among the inventions mentioned are the incandescent lamp (Edison), the FM radio (Armstrong), the microwave oven (Raytheon), the microcomputer (Altair and Apple) and the microprocessor (Intel). They point out that invitations to collaborate with the inventors of these technological breakthroughs were often turned down by larger firms.

The drawback to large firm research is that innovation in large firms becomes routinized and results in a reluctance to explore new technological fields. A wide variety of organizational studies support the idea that "inertia" within an organization increases with age and size (Hannan and Freeman 1984; Downs 1967). This inertia perpetuates innovation along established directions but prevents exploration of new opportunities and hence development of "radical" innovations. Smaller firms are more likely to possess the organizational characteristics permitting the adjustments necessary to take advantage of new opportunities. Further, a range of factors including financing, government regulations, and the motives and goals of the entrepreneurs provide the conditions for small firms that are more amenable to the exploration of diversity (Nooteboom 1994). Hence small firms are better equipped to exploit new technological opportunities through the exploration of diversity. Some support for the link between new entrants and radical innovation is provided by Henderson (1993). In a study of the photolithographic alignment equipment industry, Henderson shows that larger incumbent firms were less productive than start-up firms in exploiting radical innovations.

However, as Schumpeter (1934) noted early, start-up companies are hampered by limits to financial and human resources to support their activities. Small firms rely on regional knowledge networks for important inputs to the innovative process. The presence of spatially concentrated mutually supportive networks has been well documented in many regions of the world. Localized information sharing was common among geographically clustered firms in the steel industry in nineteenth-century England (Allen 1983). Case studies of regional clusters of small and medium-sized firms in Italy (Piore and Sabel 1984) and Baden-Württemberg in Germany (Herrigel 1993) indicate extensive interdependencies between the firms located in these regions.

More recent statistical studies have conclusively found that innovations have a strong regional character. In a recent study, Jaffe, Trajtenberg, and Henderson (1993) analyzed patent citation data pertaining to domestic university and corporate patents to test the extent of localization of knowledge spillovers. They found evidence that patents tend to be cited in the same area where the originating patents are located, even after controlling for the existing concentration of patenting activity. Similarly, Almeida and Kogut (1995) studied the spatial diffusion of technological knowledge through the analysis of important semiconductor innovations and through field interviews with engineers and scientists in the industry. Their findings indicate that knowledge remains localized in the United States and particularly in Silicon Valley.

The presence of a local network holds several advantages in resource acquisition for small firms. One of the advantages of regional networks for small firms is that locational proximity reduces the cost and increases the frequency of personal contacts and serves to build social relations. Professional relationships are often embedded in these social networks. Local social and professional networks decrease the uncertainty and costs associated with start-up activity, which encourages the provision of venture capital. The flow of information that serves as a common stock of knowledge in the region for innovations also sets the foundations for the exploration and exploitation of new knowledge by start-ups.

But why should this phenomenon of regional networking benefit smaller firms rather than larger firms? One reason is that larger firms are more self-reliant and fail to build relationships with other institutions within the region. By definition of a start-up, the personnel in a new company will have, on average, a short tenure in the company and, hence, recent employment experiences in other firms or research institutions.

More intriguing is that the paucity of resources in a small firm creates an incentive to rely upon outside sources of knowledge. In a rich ethnography of regions in the semiconductor industry, Saxenian (1994) contrasted the industrial systems of the Route 128 region (around Boston) and the Silicon Valley area (near San Francisco) to explain the comparative success of the Bay Area. She noted that the Silicon Valley region with its greater share of start-up firms is characterized by local collective learning and experimentation resulting in extensive interfirm knowledge exchange. The Route 128 region is dominated by larger firms that are more insulated from the surrounding institutions. These firms did not build relationships with other firms in that region, and this, in part, contributed to the decline of that region in recent years.

Statistical studies have confirmed the importance of external sourcing of resources by small firms. Feldman (1994) uses Small Business Administration innovation data to ascertain the importance of inputs to innovation for firms of different sizes. She finds that although large firms benefit from local innovation, for small firms the benefits are significant—small firms are two times more sensitive to local university research.

We seek to establish two important facts about innovations and start-ups. First, start-ups are unusually oriented toward the exploration of diversity by targeting less crowded technological fields. Second, their exploration has a strong local character: they are more sensitive to, and contribute more to, the innovations of spatially contiguous firms. To establish these facts, we analyze patenting and citations in the semiconductor industry.

## Research Setting: The Semiconductor Industry

Insight into the evolution of "optimal size distributions" of an industry can be gleaned in the history of the early entry and growth of start-ups into the semiconductor industry, and their subsequent relationships to a second wave of entry that commenced in the late 1970s. Technological innovation, start-up firms, and regions have all played a vital part in the development of the semiconductor industry over the last five decades. The industry originated from the invention of the first solid-state transistor at the laboratories of AT&T (Bell Labs) in New Jersey in 1947. The industry has been characterized by waves of start-up activity, each resulting in the exploration of new fields and the discovery of major innovations. Ever since William Shockley left Bell Labs to start Shockley Semiconductors in Palo Alto, California, entrepreneurship and hence start-ups have played an important role in the diffusion of knowledge and the evolution of the industry (Moore 1986). Several of Shockley's assistants left his firm and formed Fairchild Semiconductors in 1957. The newly formed Fairchild was the source of one of the most important innovations in the semiconductor industry. In 1959, Robert Noyce of Fairchild developed the "planar process" that permitted large-scale production of integrated circuits. This important advance helped launch the era of the integrated circuit. Fairchild itself spawned a host of new spin-offs. In fact, the origins of almost every firm in Silicon Valley can be traced back to Fairchild. Several of these start-ups, via successful innovation, grew into large firms, often dominating sections of the industry.

The most striking example of the process of growth through innovation is the case of Intel. Intel, one of the "Fairchildren," was started by a group of entrepreneurs in the late 1960s. Within a few years of its formation Intel introduced both the memory chip and the microprocessor—the two types of integrated circuits that came to dominate the semiconductor industry. With the growing popularity of the personal computer in the 1980s and 1990s, the demand for memory and microprocessor chips exploded. Though Intel dropped out of the memory market, the firm continued to dominate the microprocessor segment. Even today, Intel produces 70 percent of the world's microprocessors, making it the largest semiconductor manufacturer in the world.

Though larger firms came to dominate more established fields (the memory segment is dominated by large Japanese firms), new waves of start-ups continue to bring about technological changes. In the 1980s, small firms dominated innovation in the areas of application-specific integrated circuits (ASICs), high performance CMOS memory, and logic chips. As ASICs grew more popular over the last decade, many of the start-ups of the 1980s have grown rapidly. A new wave of start-ups in the middle 1990s are investigating new and emerging fields such as three-dimensional integrated circuits, voice recognition and synthesis, bioelectronics, and optoelectronics. While semiconductor start-ups continue to drive new design technologies, larger firms dominate in the manufacture of integrated circuits and the development of more mature segments of the industry. Thus, though innovation is driven by firms of all sizes, the entry and growth process of new firms continues to play an important role in new technology development.

Another remarkable aspect of the semiconductor industry is the role played by regional networks. Technology diffusion within regions has been facilitated by the culture of networking and information exchange between engineers. Managers within the industry are known to actively seek outside information useful in various stages of innovation (Saxenian 1991). Engineers at different companies share problem-solving information by discussing failed avenues of exploration; solutions are less likely to be communicated (Rogers 1982). Many of these conversations take place at social occasions. In their history of the semiconductor industry, Braun and MacDonald (1982), provide the example of a bar located close to Intel, Fairchild, Raytheon, and other semiconductor companies, which served as a place where engineers "drank, exchanged information and hired employees." Thus the prevalence of start-ups and the culture of networking make the semiconductor industry a good candidate for the study of innovativeness of small firms.

## Data and Methods

The research design is broken into two parts. The first part is oriented toward establishing that small (mostly start-up) firms are more active in the less crowded technological fields. The second part is designed to analyze whether the diffusion of small firm research activities is more localized than that of larger firms.

Two types of data are used for the analysis: (1) Patent data relating to important semiconductor design innovations, and (2) semiconductor plant location data used to identify relevant regions. By plotting the location of semiconductor plants throughout the United States, eighteen main regions of semiconductor activity were identified. The most important regions in terms of both number of plants and employment were in the Silicon Valley area and the New York–New Jersey–Pennsylvania area. Other important regions of semiconductor activity included the Boston 128 corridor, Texas (Austin), California (Los Angeles), and Arizona.[1]

In this essay, we use U.S. patent data to (1) examine the areas of technological exploration of small and large firms in the semiconductor industry and (2) to the examine geographic patterns of knowledge dissemination for these firms. The geographic characteristics of spillovers are analyzed using patent citation data relating to major patented innovations. This analysis is carried out using the case-control method. The case-control study seeks to investigate the extent to which citing patents and comparable patents (controls) differ with respect to their geographic characteristics.

## Identification of Major Innovations

Patent citation data are first used to identify important inventions. (The appendix describes patent citation data and their applicability to the semiconductor industry.) Several studies (Albert et al. 1991; Carpenter, Narin, and Woolf 1981; Narin, Noma, and Perry 1987) have shown that patent citation counts are a good indicator of the technological importance of an invention. Further, Trajtenberg (1990), in his study of CT scanners, showed that the number of citations to a patent serves as an indicator of social and economic value of the innovation. Highly cited patents tend to be of both technological and economic importance.

We first identified highly cited patents from over 400 technical classes and over 100,000 subclasses that make up the U.S. patent classification system. Since this study is concerned with patents related to semiconductor devices, the relevant classes and subclasses for semiconductors were identified using the classes specified by the U.S. Patent Office (U.S. Department of Commerce 1992). These classes, however, are not exclusive to the industry. A broad scan of the relevant semiconductor classes was undertaken and all highly cited patents (having more than 10 citations) were identified. From this broad set of patents, semiconductor design patents were identified by two electrical engineers through a review of titles, abstracts, and when necessary, complete patent documents.

In an earlier study, we identified major patents with application years in three distinct time periods (1975, 1980, and 1985).[2] The sample of relevance to this study is the 1985 sample of design patents, which consisted of 20 patents that fulfilled the criteria for selection as a major patent. This sample did not generate any patents belonging to small or start-up firms. Curiously, in spite of the apparent innovativeness of start-ups in the semiconductor industry, no major patent identified by the research design belonged to a start-up firm. Given the history of start-ups in the semiconductor industry, the result is surprising. However, in the course of the study, it became clear that start-ups were frequently active in other technological classes. As a result, we generated a second design oriented toward capturing major patents held by start-ups.

We identified all the patents belonging to any of the 176 semiconductor start-ups formed between 1977 and 1989 (Dataquest 1990). Of the 176 firms, 57 firms had significant (3 or more) patenting records. From these patents, we identified the most highly cited patents filed in the year 1985, thus creating a sample of major patents belonging to start-up firms.

This second method generated a list of 20 major patents belonging to semiconductor start-ups. As a result, we created two samples of major patents. The first sample was drawn by identifying the 20 most highly cited major patents in conventional semiconductor technological fields according the U.S. Patent Office (U.S. Department of Commerce 1992). The second sample began with start-up firms and then identified their 20 most highly cited patents. An examination of the technology (patent) classes of these innovations revealed that the major innovations were in technological fields not included in the list originally used to identify major semiconductor patents. Apparently, start-ups' major innovations belong to different fields than those dominated by larger firms.

In table 1, we report the descriptive statistics for the two samples. The patents from both samples were highly cited (about 15 citing patents per major patent). If, as explained earlier, the number of citations to a patent are an indicator of importance, major innovations from start-ups and "other" firms play a critical role in technology development.

## Citations and Controls

Localization is indicated by the joint condition that the citing patent and the major innovation belong to the same geographic region. To measure the frequency of localization, we geographically matched each set of major patents with the citing patents. However, the observed frequency of geographic coincidence of the major patent and the citing patents may reflect the distribution of patenting activity rather than the localization of spillovers.

To adjust for any bias due to this existing distribution of technological activity, we followed Jaffe et al. (1993) in the construction of a control sample. For each citing patent, we identified a corresponding control patent. This patent was identified such that the patent (technology) class was identical to that of the citing patent and the application date was as near as possible to the citing patent. The control patent thus closely resembles the citing patent in terms of technology and time of innovation. Since the control patent, however, does not cite the major patent, the frequency of geographic matches between the two reflects the existing concentration of patenting activity for a particular region. This frequency of geographic matches between the major patent and the control patent sets the baseline against which we compare the frequency of major patent-citing patent matches.

**Table 1. Descriptive Statistics**

| Sample | Number of Major Patents | Number of Citations | Mean Citations | Self Citations (%) |
|---|---|---|---|---|
| Start-ups | 20 | 298 | 14.9 | 11.4 |
| Other firms | 20 | 300 | 15 | 16 |

*Note:* Self-citations are not used in the statistical tests.

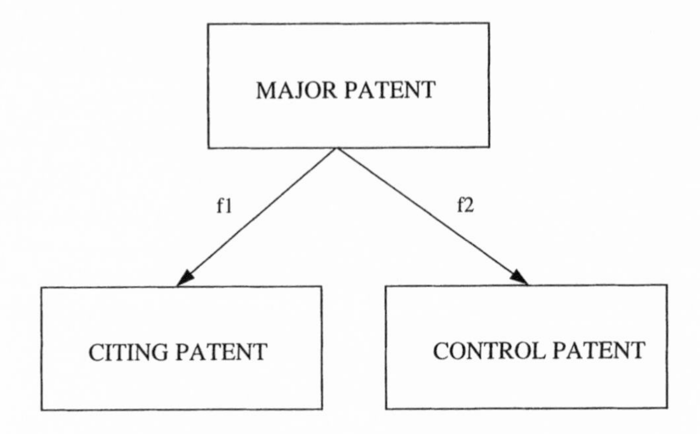


**Fig. 1. Test of localization of patent citations. fl = frequency of major-citing patent matches; f2 = frequency of major-control patent matches; null hypothesis: fl = f2.**

## Statistical Test for Localization of Spillovers

Figure 1 illustrates the design of the statistical test. Let $P_{cit}$ be the frequency probability that the major patent and citing patent are geographically matched, and $P_{con}$ be the corresponding frequency probability for the major patent-control patent match. Assuming binomial distributions, the null hypothesis is

$$H_o: P_{cit} = P_{con}$$

and the alternate hypothesis is

$$H_a: P_{cit} > P_{con}.$$

The *t*-statistic is calculated as follows

$$t = (P_{cit} - P_{con})/[(P_{cit}(1 - P_{cit}) + P_{con}(1 - P_{con})/n]0.5.$$

The *t*-statistic tests the difference between two independently drawn binomial proportions.

For both samples, $P_{cit}$, $P_{con}$, and the corresponding *t*-statistic were calculated. A positive significant value of Student's *t* indicates support of the proposition that spillovers are geographically mediated. The tests were carried out for geographic regions within the United States for both samples.

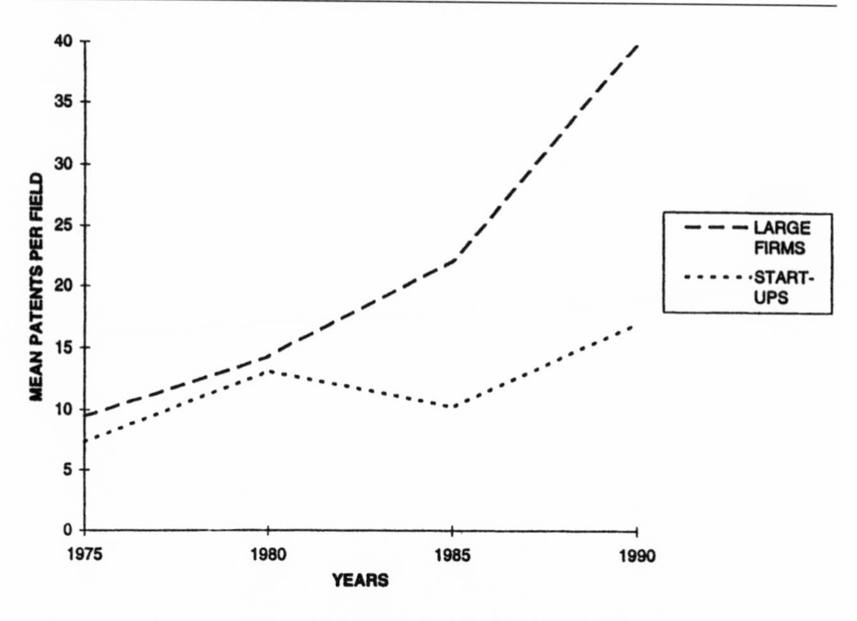


Fig. 2. **Patenting in technology fields**

## Results and Discussion

### Exploration of Technological Diversity

To examine whether start-up firms patent in less crowded fields than larger firms, we identified the technology classes in which these firms had produced major innovations. We then plotted the total number of patents granted by the U.S. Patent Office in (1) the technology classes in which the larger firms had their major patents and (2) the technology classes in which the start-up firms had their major patents. The results are shown in figure 2.

The figure reveals that start-ups produce major innovations in less crowded technological fields. Larger firms seem to concentrate in more established fields, which have a larger concentration of innovative activity.[3] For instance, established firms like Intel, Motorola, Toshiba, and Siemens dominate patenting in microprocessor and dynamic random access memory (DRAM) technologies. Smaller firms are more active in patenting in the areas of application-specific integrated circuits (ASICs), gallium arsenide, and analog integrated circuits.

We also applied the Student's *t*-test to test for significance in the differences between sample means. Table 2 reveals significant results for the 1985 and 1990 time periods but not for the 1975 and 1980 period. This analysis

**Table 2. Test of Technological Exploration: Start-ups vs. Other Firms**

| | 1975 | 1980 | 1985 | 1990 |
|---|---|---|---|---|
| Other firms—mean | 9.45 | 14.35 | 22.05 | 39.85 |
| Start-ups—mean | 7.3 | 13.2 | 10.3 | 17.05 |
| *t*-statistic | 0.54 | 0.15 | 2.6 | 3.15 |

*Note:* Mean indicates the mean number of patents per technological field in which either start-ups or "other" firms have major patents.

provides some support for the proposition that small firms are more likely to explore technologically diverse and uncrowded territories, leaving the domination of more mature technologies to larger firms.

## Geographic Localization

The sample of major patents belonging to start-up firms is also used to gauge the extent of geographic localization of knowledge pertaining to these patents. Table 3 compares the extent of localization of knowledge for start-ups and "other firms." The "number of citations" corresponds to the total number of cites for the sample less self-cites (when the major and citing patent have the same assignee). "A" and "B" are the percentage of citations and controls respectively that belong to the same geographic location as the major patent. The *t*-statistic tests the equality of the control and citing proportions as described previously.

There is a significantly higher proportion of citation matches than control matches indicating significant localization effects. The results confirm the principal findings of Jaffe et al. (1993); here, knowledge is localized for both samples but is much more significant for the start-up sample. Start-up firms are more closely tied into regional networks.

The greater localization of knowledge observed for small firms is not surprising since a large majority of new firms are located in Silicon Valley. Of the 176 start-ups founded around the world between 1977 and 1989, 55 percent were located in Silicon Valley (Dataquest 1990). Almeida and Kogut

**Table 3. Test of Localization of Knowledge: Start-ups vs. Other Firms**

| | Other Firms | Start-Ups |
|---|---|---|
| Number of citations | 147 | 264 |
| A = Citation matching % | 19.72 | 33.71 |
| B = Control matching % | 6.8 | 10.61 |
| *t*-statistic | 3.33 | 6.55 |

*Note:* Only patents from U.S. regions are used in the analysis.

**Table 4. Test of Localization of Knowledge: Silicon Valley Patents**

| | Other Firms | Start-Ups |
|---|---|---|
| Number of citations | 34 | 158 |
| A = Citation matching % | 52.9 | 53.80 |
| B = Control matching % | 14.7 | 17.72 |
| *t*-statistic | 3.64 | 7.35 |

(1995) show that Silicon Valley is unique in terms of its sociology, with extensive interfirm mobility of engineers, resulting in significant localization of design knowledge. Could the significant localization of knowledge of start-up firms be only due to the characteristics of the region (Silicon Valley) rather than the characteristics of small firms themselves?

To investigate this question, we identified the major patents from both samples that belonged to Silicon Valley and conducted localization tests on those samples (table 4). Knowledge emanating from start-up firms was more localized than for other firms. Even within Silicon Valley smaller firms appear to be more integrated into knowledge networks than larger firms. We also investigated the role of start-ups as receivers of knowledge. For every major patent belonging to a start-up firm, we identified the citing. Splitting the sample into the two categories (start-up vs. non-start-up firms), we conducted localization tests to see whether small firms were networked to other small firms locally. The results in table 5 indicate significant localization effects for both categories but again localization was more significant for start-up firms.

We then turned to understanding better how start-up firms entered into these regional networks. Much of the start-up activity in Silicon Valley is directed toward the exploitation of new ideas by an individual or a group of entrepreneurs (Rogers and Larsen 1984). Entrepreneurs use their knowledge of local suppliers, venture capitalists and other firms to further the success of their new firms. Eisenhardt and Schoonhoven (1990) showed that entrepreneurs in Silicon Valley are closely networked with venture capitalists and also with other firms in the region. Since the founders of new firms

**Table 5. Test of Localization of Knowledge: Receivers of Knowledge**

| | Other Firms | Start-Ups |
|---|---|---|
| Number of citations | 223 | 41 |
| A = Citation matching % | 26.91 | 70.73 |
| B = Control matching % | 9.87 | 14.63 |
| *t*-statistic | 4.76 | 6.23 |

play an important role in the networking activities of new firms, one would expect that previous experience in the region where the start-up is located would be an important prerequisite to successful networking activity.

To assess the role played by founders of semiconductor firms, we examined the geographic origins of entrepreneurs. Table 6 presents the results of phone interviews of 76 start-up firms (120 firms were contacted, for a response rate of 63 percent). Over 88 percent of the founders were employed in the same region prior to the formation of the start-up. As can be seen, previous local experience of entrepreneurs influences the location of start-up activity and therefore the firm's networking potential.

## Conclusion: Small Firms and Globalization

This essay offers two reasons for the innovativeness of small firms. Small firms enter as start-ups based on their promise to explore technologically diverse fields, and they are tied into local knowledge networks that support their exploration. If successful, start-up firms build upon this knowledge and branch into new fields. However, this subsequent diversification is linked to the richness of the technological opportunities. In fact, Kogut and Kim (1996) found that start-ups that began in very narrow technological fields developed little capacity to support subsequent diversification.

We have, consequently, a sketch of an industry that is driven by the exploration of new technological fields. This exploration is frequently carried out by small firms that are linked in dense local networks, to which

**Table 6. Geographic Origins of Start-Up Founders**

| U.S. Region | Number of Firms | Matches Number | Matches (%) |
|---|---|---|---|
| California—Silicon Valley | 44 | 38 | 86 |
| California—Los Angeles and San Diego | 9 | 8 | 89 |
| New York/New Jersey/Pennsylvania | 3 | 3 | 100 |
| Texas | 2 | 2 | 100 |
| Massachusetts | 4 | 4 | 100 |
| Oregon/Washington | 4 | 3 | 75 |
| Colorado | 5 | 5 | 100 |
| Other | 4 | 3 | 75 |
| Total | 75 | 66 | 88 |

*Note:* "Number of firms" indicates the total number of start-up responses per region. "Matches" indicates the number of firms for which the founders had worked in the same region immediately prior to the founding of the new firm.

large firms also belong. When successful, the start-ups prosper and grow. No wonder there is no easy relationship between size and innovation.

There is an interesting policy issue embedded in this discussion, for the financial constraints on small firms often make them vulnerable to acquisition. In fact, in the 1980s, 20 percent of all start-ups involved in ASIC products (application-specific integrated circuits) were acquired. The twin conditions of being small and holding knowledge that is local and not internationally diffused would seem to make these start-up firms vulnerable to foreign acquisition.

This question provides an interesting insight into the relationship among small and large firms. Kogut et al. (1993) found that cooperative relationships in the semiconductor industry were structured into national industrial networks. However, American small firms were tightly networked with each other and with American large firms. In turn, the American large firm was linked not only to the local small firm network, but also to large companies from other regions, especially from Japan. The cooperative pattern in the United States shows, not surprisingly given the preceding results, a dense national small firm network, with larger firms bridging nations.

An alternative to cooperation is acquisition. Small firms in regions such as Silicon Valley are attractive acquisition targets of larger firms seeking technological knowledge inputs. Over the last decade, several firms including Philips, Thomson-CSF, Toshiba, Sony, Samsung, and a number of other electronic firms, have bought into local knowledge networks by acquiring semiconductor start-ups. Almeida (1996) shows that these foreign firms in U.S. regions use local regional knowledge extensively in their innovative activities.

This discussion, besides its relevance to policy debates over foreign technological acquisition, is important in underlining the problem in focusing solely on the individual firm. Innovation is an activity that shifts the size distribution of firms. It is closely linked to the general progress of science and technology in society. For small firms, innovation is more often than not the product of a firm's efforts to benefit from its own research and from a local network of entrepreneurs and innovators. The difficulty of re-creating such networks, as evident in Silicon Valley, is certainly one of the leading reasons why the distribution of innovations varies among regions and countries.

## APPENDIX: PATENT DATA AND THE SEMICONDUCTOR INDUSTRY

This study uses semiconductor patent data to analyze the extent of localization of knowledge spillovers in this industry. Though some firms may choose not to patent innovations, patenting in the semiconductor industry is commonly practiced and is indeed a vital part of maintaining technological competitiveness. Firms may patent for a variety of reasons. The factors that motivate a firm to patent include:

1. Patents establish intellectual property rights that often become an important revenue source (during the late 1980s Texas Instruments earned over a billion dollars from patent royalties);

2. Patent portfolios are used by firms as bargaining chips to prevent or to fight legal battles;

3. Patents facilitate licensing and cross-licensing which often serves as an important source of learning for the firm; and

4. Interviews with headhunting firms and engineers revealed that patents are valuable to individual engineers and researchers as indicators of personal technological expertise.

Recent government actions have increased the protection for intellectual capital supplied by the patent system and thereby increased the incentive to patent. In 1982, Congress created the U.S. Court of Appeals for the Federal Circuit in Washington, DC, specifically for the purpose of hearing patent cases. This action significantly increased the protection provided by patents.

## NOTES

We are grateful to Jerome Romano for his research assistance. This essay was presented at the seminar on Small and Medium-Sized Enterprises and the Global Economy at the University of Maryland at College Park, October 20, 1995.

1. Dataquest, a private research firm located in San Jose, California, and County Business Patterns (U.S. Department of Commerce publication) were the main sources of plant location data.

2. The major innovations, represented by heavily cited patents, were identified in cooperation with CHI Research, a private research firm. Citing patents and control patents were identified through the use of the on-line patent data base provided in the LEXPAT file on LEXIS.

3. We used the mean number (for the twenty technological classes) of patents in a given year to capture the extent of patenting in the fields. Ideally we would have liked to produce an indicator of the age of the technological fields in which smaller and larger firms patent, but the patent classification system does not permit this.

## REFERENCES


Acs, Zoltan, and David Audretsch. 1990. *Innovation and Small Firms.* Cambridge: MIT Press.

Albert, M. B., D. Avery, F. Narin, and P. McAllister. 1991. "Direct Validation of Citation Counts as Indicators of Industrially Important Patents." *Research Policy* 20:251–59.

Allen, Robert. 1983. "Collective Invention." *Journal of Economic Behavior and Organization* 4:1–24.

Almeida, Paul. 1996. "Knowledge Sourcing by Foreign Multinationals: Patent Citation Analysis in the US Semiconductor Industry." *Strategic Management Journal* 17:155–65.

Almeida, Paul, and Bruce Kogut. 1995. "Technology and Geography: The Localization of Knowledge and the Mobility of Patent Holders." Working Paper, The Huntsman Center for Global Competition and Innovation, The Wharton School, Philadelphia.

Bound, J. C., C. Cummins, Z. Griliches, B. H. Hall, and A. Jaffe. 1984. "Who Does R&D and Who Patents." In Z. Griliches, ed., *R&D, Patents and Productivity.* Chicago: University Press.

Braun, Ernest, and Stuart MacDonald. 1982. *Revolution in Miniature.* 2d ed. New York: Cambridge University Press.

Carpenter, Mark, Francis Narin, and Patricia Woolf. 1981. "Citation Rates to Technologically Important Patents." *World Patent Information* 3 (4): 160–63.

Cohen, W., and S. Klepper. 1996. "The Trade-off between Firm Size and Diversity in the Pursuit of Technological Progress." *Small Business Economics* 4 (1): 1–14.

Cohen, Wes, and Richard Levin. 1989. "Innovation and Market Structure." In *Handbook of Industrial Organization,* ed. Richard Schmalensee and Robert Willig. Amsterdam: North Holland.

Dataquest. 1990. *A Decade of Semiconductor Start-ups.* San Jose, CA.

Downs, A. 1967. *Inside Bureaucracy.* Boston: Little, Brown.

Eisenhardt, K. M., and C. B. Schoonhoven. 1990. "Organizational Growth: Founding Teams Strategy and Environment and Growth among US Semiconductor Ventures 1978–1988." *Administrative Science Quarterly* 35 (3): 504–29.

Feldman, Maryann. 1994. "Knowledge Complementarity and Innovation." *Small Business Economics* 6 (5): 363–72.

Grefsheim, S., J. Franklin, and D. Cunningham. 1991. "Biotechnology Awareness Study, Part 1: Where Scientists Get their Information." *Bulletin of the Medical Library Association* 79:36–44.

Hannan, Michael, and John Freeman. 1984. "Structural Inertia and Organizational Change." *American Sociological Review* 49:149–64.

Henderson, R. 1993. "Underinvestment and Incompetence as Responses to Radical Innovation: Evidence from the Photolithographic Alignment Equipment Industry." *RAND Journal of Economics* 24 (2): 248–70.

Herrigel, Gary. 1993. "Large Firms, Small Firms, and the Governance of Flexible Specialization: The Case of Baden Wurttemberg and Socialized Risk." In Bruce Kogut, ed., *Country Competitiveness.* New York: Oxford University Press.

Jaffe, A., M. Trajtenberg, and R. Henderson. 1993. "Geographic Localization of Knowledge Spillovers as Evidenced by Patent Citations." *Quarterly Journal of Economics* 108 (3): 577–98.

Jewkes, J., D. Sawers, and R. Stillerman. 1958. *The Sources of Invention.* London: St. Martin's Press.

Kogut, Bruce, and Dong-Jae Kim. 1996. "Diversification and Platform Technologies." *Organization Science* 7:283–301.

Kogut, Bruce, Gordon Walker, Weijian Shan, and Dong-Jae Kim. 1993. "Platform Technologies and National Industrial Networks." In John Hagedoorn, ed., *Internationalization of Corporate Technology Strategy.* Cheltham: Edward Elgan.

McKenney, James, Michael Zack, and Victor Doherty. 1992. "Complementary Communication Media: A Comparison of Electronic Mail and Face-To-Face Communication in a Programming Team." In Nitin Nohria and Robert Eccles, eds., *Networks and Organizations.* Boston: Harvard Business School Press.

Moore, Gordon E. 1986. "Entrepreneurship and Innovation: The Electronics Industry." In R. Landau and N. Rosenberg, eds., *Positive Sum Strategy.* Washington, DC: National Academy Press.

Narin, F., E. Noma, and R. Perry. 1987. "Patents as Indicators of Technological Strength." *Research Policy* 16:143–55.

Nooteboom, Bart. 1994. "Innovation and Diffusion in Small Firms: Theory and Evidence." *Small Business Economics* 6 (5): 327–48.

Pavitt, K. 1984. "Sectoral Patterns of Ethnological Change." *Research Policy* 13:343–73.

Pavitt, K., M. Robson, and J. Townsend. 1987. "The Size Distribution of Innovating Firms in the U.K.: 1945–1983." *Journal of Industrial Economics* 55:291–316.

Piore, M., and C. Sabel. 1984. *The Second Industrial Divide: Possibilities for Prosperity.* New York: Basic Books.

Rogers, Everett. 1982. "Information Exchange and Technological Innovation." In D. Sahal, ed., *The Transfer and Utilization of Technical Knowledge,* 105–23. Boston: Lexington Books.

Rogers, Everett, and Judith Larson. 1984. *Silicon Valley Fever.* New York: Basic Books.

Saxenian, AnnaLee. 1991. "The Origins and Dynamics of Production Networks in Silicon Valley." *Research Policy* 20:423–37.

———. 1994. *Regional Advantage.* Cambridge: Harvard University Press.

Scherer, F. M. 1984. *Innovation and Growth: Schumpeterian Perspectives.* Cambridge: MIT Press.

Scherer, F. M., and D. Ross. 1990. *Industrial Market Structure and Economic Performance.* Boston: Houghton Mifflin.

Schumpeter, J. A. 1934. *Theory of Economic Development.* Boston: Harvard University Press.

———. 1943. *Capitalism, Socialism and Democracy.* London: Unwin.

Trajtenberg, Manuel. 1990. "A Penny for Your Quotes." *RAND Journal of Economics* 21 (1): 172–87.

U.S. Department of Commerce, Patent and Trademark Office. 1992. *Technology Profile Report: Semiconductors.* U.S. Department of Commerce, Washington, DC.

# The Production, Transfer, and Spillover of Technology

## Comparing Large and Small Multinationals as Technology Producers

*Lorraine Eden, Edward Levitas, and Richard J. Martinez*

It is now a cliché to say that multinational enterprises (MNEs) produce, control, and own most of the world's technology. The various issues of the UNCTC's *World Investment Report* have provided extraordinary detail about the technological activities of MNEs.[1] For example, we know that in the OECD countries about 80 percent of R&D activities of private firms take place in firms with more than 10,000 employees. Between 75 and 80 percent of all private R&D expenditures worldwide are accounted for by multinationals (Dunning 1993, 290).

In addition, most technology production by MNEs takes place at home. U.S. multinationals, for example, perform only about 13 percent of their R&D offshore. In the late 1980s, over 80 percent of all R&D expenditures occurred in five countries: the United States, Japan, France, the United Kingdom, and West Germany (Dunning 1993, 300). In instances where R&D facilities are located abroad, such action is generally pursued to customize products for local markets or meet local content requirements (OTA 1994, 76).

Technology transfer among multinational organizations, whether they be large or small, has also been the subject of much research (Buckley 1995; Dunning 1988; Kogut and Zander 1995; McFetridge 1995; UNCTC 1992). In general, this body of research has led to the conclusion that organizations engage in the transfer of technology in order to profit directly from the transfer (as in licensing arrangements), profit indirectly from the dissemination of the product or process (for example, establishing industry standards), or in order to enable foreign affiliates to utilize organization-specific technologies in their operations.

Further, technology transfer from MNEs to host countries is the primary mechanism by which developing countries receive technology (Caves 1996; Dunning 1993; UNCTC 1992). Most royalties, license and management fees—forms of payment for technology—are in-house payments, flowing from MNE subsidiaries to their parent firms. For example, over 90 percent of technology payments to foreigners made by Canadian subsidiaries of U.S. multinationals are intrafirm transfers to their U.S. parents (Eden forthcoming, chap. 4).

The preceding statistical picture suggests that multinationals are, sine qua non, the world's technology producers. In this essay, we review the literature on MNEs and technology, focusing specifically on three aspects: (1) technology as a firm-specific advantage, (2) the costs of technology transfer, and (3) technology spillovers. In each case, we outline current views and debates in the field about the role played by large multinationals in technology production. We then compare the ability of MNEs to produce and profit from technology with that of small and medium-sized enterprises (SMEs). We conclude that, although SMEs face certain constraints on technological productivity that their larger counterparts do not face, this does not preclude SMEs from contributing, often significantly, to technological advancement. However, MNEs are likely to remain synonymous with knowledge production.

## Technology as a Firm-Specific Advantage

The literature on multinational enterprises and foreign direct investment (FDI) suggests that knowledge is the key source of ownership or firm-specific advantage (FSA) held by multinationals. The MNE goes abroad to earn rents on its store of knowledge, and the creation and exploitation of that knowledge is the main reason for the success and growth of the multinational over time (see, for example, Caves 1996, chap. 1; Dunning 1988, 1993, chaps. 11 and 12; Johnson 1970). Given this focus on knowledge, three perspectives describing how knowledge determines the expansion tendencies of MNEs have emerged.

According to the *public goods perspective,* knowledge is conceptualized as a public intermediate good owned by the firm that can be transferred at zero (or negligible) marginal cost to various units within the MNE (Johnson 1970). Given the ease of transfer, a critical concern for the MNE is the potential for unintended transfer to, and expropriation of that knowledge by, competitors. As such, the public goods perspective suggests that MNEs will internalize transactions when transacting in the external market poses a significant risk of knowledge appropriation by competitors that would dissipate the MNE's knowledge-based FSA. Such cases are likely where property rights to the knowledge have not been assigned or are not effective (for example, countries without patent protection).

The *internalization perspective* suggests that the decision by the MNE to organize outside of its home country rests in the costs of transferring knowledge to those distant locations. While this perspective recognizes the public good aspect of knowledge, the focus is more on the weight of bureaucratic costs (costs of hierarchical organization) relative to transaction costs (costs of transacting through the market) in determining expansion. MNEs will internalize divisions in host countries at that point where the costs of increased bureaucratization are just outweighed by the transaction costs associated with market contracting (Hennart 1991; Buckley and Casson 1976; Rugman 1981).

The *technological competence perspective* also attaches primacy to knowledge in determining the expansion activities of MNEs (Cantwell 1989, 1991). This perspective is different from the other two in that the importance of technological competence in determining an MNE's competitive advantage is stressed over knowledge transfer costs. In this framework, the MNE is not simply a mechanism through which costs are reduced but rather a vehicle through which knowledge is recombined (à la Schumpeter 1934) to produce and subsequently exploit new and valuable innovations (Kogut and Zander 1992, 1993, 1995). A firm's facility in accomplishing recombination and exploitation is unique to that firm. As such, that knowledge remains firm-specific or *tacit.*

These three perspectives are reviewed in more detail below.

## The Public Goods Perspective

The OLI, or eclectic, paradigm developed by John Dunning (1988) suggests that MNEs choose their markets and structures according to three factors: ownership (O) or firm-specific advantages or competencies, locational (L) advantages inherent in particular geographic areas, and internalization (I) advantages derived from conducting transactions hierarchically rather than in the open market. In the OLI paradigm, ownership advantages are the key source of the MNE's competitive advantage in foreign markets.

Firm-specific advantages arise from "privileged possession of intangible assets" and advantages from common governance of crossborder activities (Dunning 1988, 79). These advantages have four characteristics: (1) the firm owns or can appropriate the assets or their services; (2) the assets differ in productivity from comparable assets possessed by competing firms; (3) they are mobile between national markets in which the MNE competes; (4) they may be depreciable or augmentable but their life spans are not short relative to the firm's investment horizon (Caves 1996). The traditional view of FSAs suggests that the primary advantage an MNE brings to foreign markets is its possession of superior knowledge; that is, its most important proprietary asset is technology or knowledge.[2] Once technology is produced, it generates income through sales of goods or services embodying the technology.

Since Hymer's 1960 dissertation on the monopolistic advantages of the MNE (Hymer 1976 [1960]), a central issue in the theory of foreign direct investment has been the nature of FSAs and their transfer across borders. FSAs are seen as proprietary assets that the firm can use but may not necessarily be able to transfer to external parties. In order for the assets to be proprietary, either the firm must hold legal title to their use, or the assets cannot be easily copied or appropriated by other firms. That is, the benefits derivable from the use of FSAs remain the exclusive domain of the possessing firm. Because foreign markets offer the opportunity to earn additional rents over and above those in the home market, FSAs provide a rationale for expansion into foreign markets (the "why go abroad?" question in the OLI paradigm).

According to this perspective, technology (or knowledge) created and used within MNEs often has the characteristics of a public good, so it is difficult for the MNE to appropriate all the returns expected from its use (Johnson 1970). Public goods have two characteristics: jointness in consumption[3] and nonexcludability.[4] As a public good, knowledge is easy to transfer but hard to protect. The twin characteristics of jointness and nonexcludability imply that the private market cannot efficiently price knowledge. Transfer through the external market will be difficult to price because of the high probability of free riding and opportunistic behavior.

Patents provide the MNE with some relief from the second characteristic, nonexcludability, by giving the firm a property right to knowledge. However, not all forms of knowledge are patentable, and patents are not a perfect panacea for nonexcludability. Protecting the knowledge advantages of the MNE from free riding and opportunistic behavior by possible competitors is therefore a key to ensuring the long-run competitive advantage of the firm. As a result, the firm will choose to transfer technology primarily through wholly owned subsidiaries rather than use external methods. Because technology which is relatively public has the jointness characteristic, the marginal cost of transfer within the MNE is low or zero. Thus the internal mobility of knowledge within the MNE, together with the need to prevent its dissipation to outsiders, implies that production and transfer of this type of technology will take place primarily within multinationals.

The publicness of knowledge therefore provides a rationale for the multinational's preference for wholly owned subsidiaries as the vehicle for transferring technology to foreign countries. That is, FDI via wholly owned subsidiaries is the transfer of the intermediate good—technology that embodies an MNE's firm-specific advantage—to host countries.

### The Internalization Perspective

Whereas the focus of the public goods perspective is on the MNE's *possession* of unique knowledge, the internalization perspective is distinct in its concentration on the factors affecting the *transfer* of that knowledge (Buckley and Casson 1976; Hennart 1991; Rugman 1981, 1986). For example, Hood and Young (1979, 56) suggest that, from the internalization perspective, "it is not the possession of a unique asset *per se* that gives a firm its advantage. Rather it is the process of internalizing that asset as opposed to selling it to a foreign producer which gives the MNE its unique advantage." Internalization decisions therefore rest on the relative weights of bureaucratic and transaction costs. The MNE internalizes these transactions as long as the costs of hierarchical organization are outweighed by the costs of knowledge transfer via the market mechanism.

Such internalization considerations arise as markets for the efficient transfer of knowledge fail. Ideally, in neoclassical theory, ambiguities in the valuing of a good are precluded as all information regarding a good's exchange value is imputed in its market price. In the international context, however, markets for knowledge fail as "there is no simple interaction of supply and demand to set a market price" (Rugman 1981, 41). As such, firms intending to sell their knowledge resources in international settings may find the appropriation of associated returns difficult. Conflicting interests among transacting parties may impede the establishment of appropriate transfer prices. Furthermore, because of the scarcity and value of knowledge and technology assets, the MNE may be subject to opportunism in dealing with external parties that seek to expropriate those assets. In these cases, internalization theory suggests that the MNE will internalize the utilization, exploitation, and transfer of knowledge rather than risk expropriation through the market mechanism.

### The Technological Competence Perspective

Cantwell (1991, 50) suggests that "technological competence . . . because it consists of those elements of a firm's technology which are distinctive, is never itself transferred through trade or copied exactly through spillovers to other firms." Technological competence, rather, is unique to each firm. It is tacit, being largely incomprehensible to competitors. This knowledge resides in the shared norms or routines of the firm's employees (Nelson and Winter 1982) and the ability of those employees to reconfigure those routines (that is, combinative capabilities per Kogut and Zander 1992) to produce novel knowledge. Whereas patents of more codifiable knowledge may provide temporary FSAs to the firm (that is, they can be bought, sold, and used by others at a cost), tacit knowledge is much more difficult to imitate.

The development of tacit knowledge is viewed as a function of the evolutionary development of the firm (Nelson and Winter 1982; Kogut and Zander 1995; Teece 1988). As a firm travels through economic space, it confronts numerous environmental stimuli. As it attempts to utilize its resources in order to profit from these environmental conditions, the firm gains an increased cognizance of its strengths and weaknesses. Combining and utilizing resources in various ways will prove profitable in some instances and useless in others. The firm will begin to recognize the value of these combinations and will develop stylized procedures with which to confront novel stimuli (Nelson and Winter 1982). Furthermore, the competent firm will develop an ability to reconstitute routines in order to counter their obsolescence. These combinative capabilities (Kogut and Zander 1992) allow for the destruction of obsolete knowledge and its reconstitution into new and valuable knowledge.

As such, tacit knowledge is acquired through "learning-by-doing" (Stiglitz 1987) or "learning-by-using" (Rosenberg 1982) and, therefore, mere observation of firms possessing such knowledge will not lead to its acquisition by knowledge-deficient firms. It is "acquired only experientially and transferred by demonstration, by personal instruction, and by the provision of expert services" (McFetridge 1995, 413, citing Dasgupta and David 1994). Thus, aspiring imitators, to some degree, must "recreate" history (Arthur 1988) in order to acquire this knowledge.

Since tacit knowledge cannot be exactly copied by other firms it is effectively rival, at least to unrelated parties, in the sense that the cost of extending provision to one more user is high. Therefore the more tacit the technology, the more likely that it will be transferred within the MNE hierarchy to wholly owned subsidiaries; whereas the more codified and teachable the technology, the more likely that third-party routes will be used (Kogut and Zander 1993). That is, complexity increases the probability of internal transfer.

These conclusions may seem somewhat paradoxical. In the public goods perspective, FDI through wholly owned subsidiaries (the hierarchy) was perceived to be the MNE's preferred route to prevent dissipation of the potential rents from knowledge production. In the more recent literature, it is the private characteristic of tacit knowledge that is the core competency of the MNE, and it is the difficulty of providing this knowledge to recipients that leads the MNE to choose the hierarchy over the market. So, publicness favored the hierarchy over the market in the traditional view (to lessen the risk of dissipation of the firm's FSAs through technology spillovers and opportunistic behavior). More recently, the common view is that tacitness (privateness) is the justification for the hierarchy (internal transfers reduce the costs of learning-by-doing, tacitness keeps the core competence of the MNE from dissipating). We explore the paradox later in our examination of the costs of technology transfer.

Yet, an important limitation on the returns to the MNE from its FSAs derives from the associated costs of transaction, which include the costs of search, enforcement, bargaining, and opportunism, as well as provision costs and dissipation costs. These will be discussed in more detail.

## Multinationals and Technology Transfer

The technology transfer process involves the acquisition, assimilation, diffusion, and development of technology (Tung 1994; Caves 1996). Technology can be transferred through formal market means or informal, nonmarket mechanisms; the latter can be voluntary or involuntary (Kokko 1992). Demonstration effects, the movement of skilled workers from one firm to another firm, and supplier-buyer linkages are all types of informal mechanisms by which knowledge is diffused. The role of the technology producer can be active or passive in the technology transfer process. For example, trade in finished goods can lead to reverse engineering; in such cases the knowledge generator is a passive actor in the technology diffusion process. On the other hand, joint ventures, licensing arrangements, and other forms of strategic alliances can lead to active participation in technology transfer.

However accomplished, technology transfer involves several types of costs for the producer. Figure 1 outlines four different, but interrelated, costs of technology transfer. The first cost type is the *transfer costs* of making a market in an uncertain world (Casson 1982). These include costs of search, negotiating a contract, monitoring and enforcing the contract. Internalization theory argues that transfer costs are higher for external transfers than for transfers through the hierarchy (Rugman 1986).

The second category of costs are the risks and *costs of opportunistic behavior* by the transacting parties, as each attempts to alter the terms of the bargain in its favor. As uncertainty increases, so does opportunism. Because

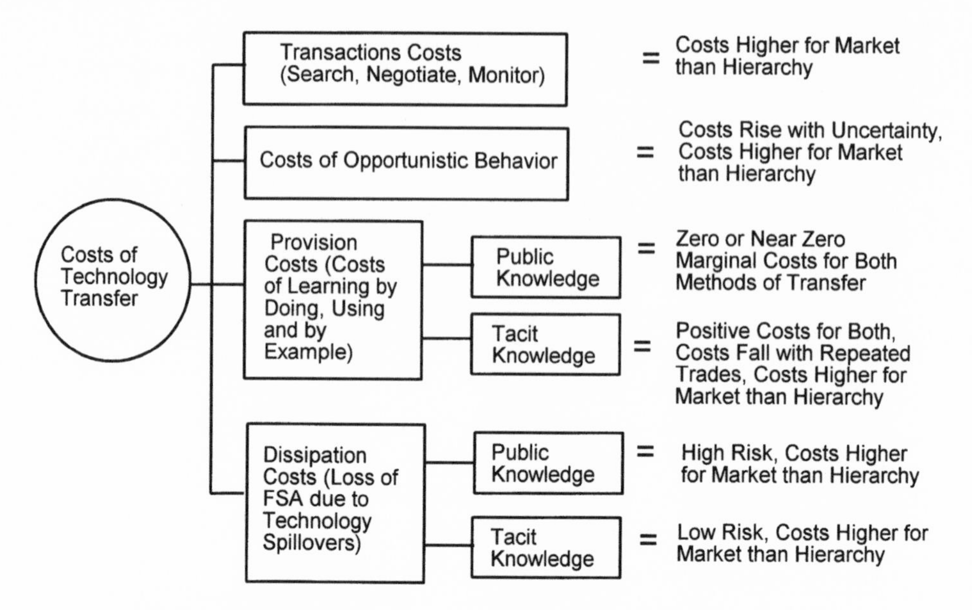


**Fig. 1. Market vs. hierarchy: Which method has higher technology transfer costs?**

knowledge is often impacted, both parties are reluctant to reveal too much information for fear of giving away an advantage (Hamel 1991; Johnson 1970). In general, technology transfer within the hierarchy should be less subject to such pressures than external transfers.

The third category is *provision costs,* that is, those identified by Teece (1977), Cantwell (1991), and Kogut and Zander (1993) referring to the costs of providing knowledge or technology to other entities, such as subsidiaries, affiliates, or external organizations. For public technology, these provision costs are approximately zero, whereas for tacit knowledge, provision costs can be substantial. Since provision costs depend on knowledge of routines and fall with repeated trades, one would expect such costs, for tacit knowledge, to be less within the hierarchy than through the market. For pure public goods, provision costs should be near zero for both methods. Note that high provision costs should be seen as a benefit to the MNE if the firm wishes to protect knowledge from diffusion outside the hierarchy. That is, the high cost of learning-by-doing suggests that unintended transfers provide minimum benefit to third parties. On the other hand, if the MNE does want to sell or lease its technology on the private market, high provision costs mean substantial costs must be incurred in terms of codifying knowledge, providing on-site technical experts, and so on.

The last category is *dissipation costs,* that is, the risk of loss of the MNE's firm-specific advantage. For example, technology spillovers to competing firms can reduce the rents from knowledge production. This risk is highest with public knowledge where the appropriability regime is weak since it is difficult for the technology producer to protect its investment from free riders (Teece 1987).[5] Dissipation costs imply that technology transfer has quasi-congestion costs in the sense that extending consumption to an additional user reduces the benefits to the original user (that is, providing benefits to *Y* means lower returns to *X*). Dissipation costs are linked with opportunistic costs in that, as uncertainty increases, the risks of opportunism and of dissipation both increase.

The public goods perspective has been particularly concerned with the last of these four types of technology transfer costs, that is, the dissipation costs associated with knowledge as a public good. Discussions of tacit knowledge as the core competence of the MNE stress mostly the third category of costs: those of provision (costs of learning-by-doing, -using, and -example) associated with tacit knowledge. Whether the knowledge dynamics of MNEs is affected most by the publicness or the tacitness of knowledge therefore depends on one's view of the size and significance of knowledge spillovers (how tight is the appropriability regime protecting knowledge from dissipation?), and the size and significance of the tacitness of knowledge (how costly is it to disseminate knowledge between firms?). We next turn to knowledge spillovers and the appropriability regime.

## Multinationals and Technology Spillovers

Spillovers, or externalities, are one of the most important ways that MNE technology is transferred to host countries. A technology spillover occurs when the activities of one firm lead to improvements in the technology or productivity of another firm such that the first firm cannot capture all the quasi rents created by its productive activities. Technology spillovers are informal, nonmarket transfers that occur involuntarily.

### The Nature of Technology Spillovers

Some of the ways that MNE technology can spill over to host country firms include:

local firms attempt to copy the MNE's product or process technologies (the *demonstration effect*);

backward and forward linkages between the MNE and its suppliers and buyers facilitate *learning-by-doing* by the local firms, creating a mechanism that reduces the provision costs of technology transfer;

*training of local employees* by the MNE provides a more highly skilled labor pool for other firms, and a potential source of new start-up firms, thus creating an external benefit for other firms; and

entry of an MNE generates more competition within an industry so local firms are forced to use existing technology more efficiently or to upgrade their technology in order to remain competitive (what Kokko [1992, 25] describes as the *competition effect*).

We next briefly review each of these methods.

The *demonstration effect* occurs as reduced geographic and operational proximity increases information flow among firms and facilitates learning by the incumbent firms. Before a technology is widely known, lack of information about its benefits and costs implies uncertainty and may discourage existing firms from adopting the technology. Technology should spread most easily when the producer and potential user are already in contact so that linkages already exist. Like the flu bug in the winter, technology diffusion happens easiest when the parties are geographically and operationally proximate. This contagion effect suggests that diffusion should be faster the closer the proximity and the larger the share of the MNE's technology in the local base.

*Learning-by-doing* occurs as linkages among firms force all firms to (attempt to) adopt common routines, industry norms, acquisitions standards, and so forth. Such conformity, on the surface, will reduce costs of transaction as exchange is governed by widely shared procedures (thus, new procedures do not have to be created for each transaction). However, at a more abstract level, conformity will cause technologically deficient firms to operate in manners similar to those firms possessing valuable technologies. As such, technologically deficient firms may be forced to mimic the actions of technologically superior firms, resulting in experiential learning by the former.

Furthermore, as suggested by Almeida and Kogut (1995), spillovers may occur as technologically superior firms *train local employees.* Once trained, these employees may be subsequently hired by technologically inferior firms and, thus, may provide these firms with superior technology. Further, highly trained local employees may feel compelled to apply their newfound expertise to entrepreneurial ventures that further diffuse the knowledge throughout local markets.

The *competition effect* arises from increased competition occasioned by the entry of the MNE into a host country. Such entry puts pressure on existing firms threatened with loss of market share. Their response may be to use existing technology more efficiently or to upgrade, either following the entrant or pursuing their own technology track/paradigm.[6]

It should be noted that technology spillovers are an implicit cost to the firm since they represent benefits that are not fully appropriated by the producing firm—benefits that could have been earned if the regime of appropriability had been more effective. Thus the total productive volume of technology by the MNE may be reduced by the existence of technology spillovers (Caves 1996, 181). That is, recognizing the potential for incomplete appropriation, MNEs may underinvest in technology generation or may erect such strict barriers to diffusion that even internal transfer of technology is hampered. In addition, technology spillovers can provide *recipients* with the ability to compete directly against the MNE, thus providing further impetus to reduce technology production.[7]

## Technology Spillovers and the Appropriability Regime

How high is the risk of technology spillovers? Figure 2 shows that the risk varies inversely with the tightness of the appropriability regime protecting the firm's technology assets, that is, how well the property rights regime protects asset holders.

First, the simplest, most basic method of deterring spillovers is through the granting of property rights to the technology (for example, patents, copyrights). This, in theory, allows the producing firm to be compensated for its innovative efforts and expense before legal diffusion of the technology becomes widespread. Second, even without ownership of the technology, expropriation by competitors may be prevented if the producing firm owns complementary and/or co-specialized assets that are necessary to realize the full value of the diffused technology. In this case, risk of dissipation is attenuated if, for example, the cost faced by imitators to build such assets is exorbitant (Teece 1987). Third, operating technologies employed by the firm may be partially composed of a tacit element. Firm-specific routines (Nelson and Winter 1982) and combinative capabilities (Kogut and Zander 1992) may guide the process through which technologies are exploited by the possessing firm. Thus, even if a portion of the firm's technology is derived by relatively codifiable knowledge, the ability of other firms to acquire a firm's entire portfolio of knowledge will be limited by codifiability constraints. If the tacit component of knowledge is high, the MNE can still maintain a tight appropriability regime and deter spillovers.

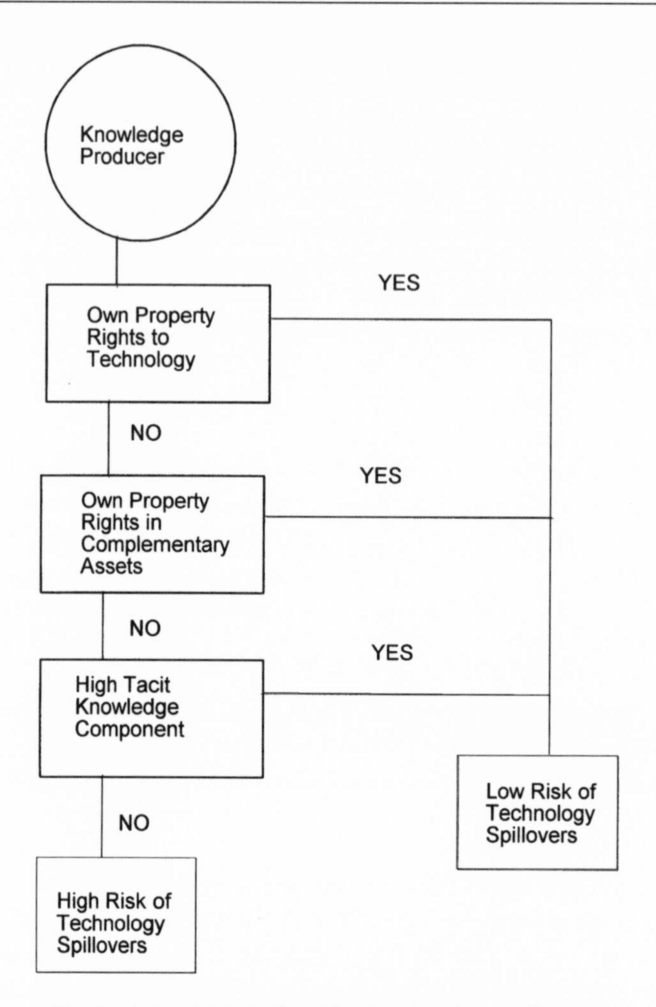


**Fig. 2. How high is the risk of technology spillovers?**

The implication of figure 2 is that the tightness of the appropriability regime, whether derived from property rights or tacitness, is another key to the success and growth of the multinational enterprise. It is the proprietary assets that create value for the firm, and these assets "may possess either the limitless capacities of public goods (the strict intangibles) or the flexible capacities of the firm's repertory of routines" (Caves 1996, 4).

One ex post measure of the tightness of the appropriability regime is the existence and location of technology spillovers. Evidence on technology spillovers has come from a variety of sources (Caves 1996; Dunning 1993; Kokko 1992). Some authors have looked at the increase in total factor productivity in the host country after the entry of foreign multinationals, focusing on the link between R&D expenditures and economic growth. Others have looked for new linkages, backward and forward, between the MNE and host country firms. Still others have investigated the impact on efficiency of firms in an industry as a result of new entry.[8] Difficulties in measuring technology spillovers may lead to serious under- or overestimation of their size; hence the interest in the work of Jaffe et al. (1993) and Almeida and Kogut (1995), who have used patent data to determine the size and the location of technology spillovers, to which we now turn.

## The Localization of Technology Spillovers

Technology spillovers can be measured using patent data. A patent is a "property right in the commercial use of a device" (Jaffe et al. 1993, 580). Patent statistics have often been used to proxy for technology because the statistics are readily available over long periods and in great detail. They also capture knowledge activities in and outside of R&D departments (Patel and Pavitt 1991).

Patents represent knowledge "which can be articulated, codified, and legally enforceable in their protection" (Almeida and Kogut 1995, 4). They have a double-barreled effect: (1) they convey a temporary monopoly on the patent holder and (2) they disclose information to the general public about the technology in codified form. That is, patents benefit the patent holder because they convey a property right on which the firm can earn rents; the scope of the patent is defined in the description of the patented product or process.

However, patent protection is imperfect (Levin et al. 1987) and the process of obtaining a patent discloses information that can be used to imitate the patented technology either illegally or via carefully considered substitute, but similar, processes. Successful imitation dissipates the rents the original technology producer can earn from its investment and thus reduces the value of the patent to the original firm. The first impact of a patent therefore reduces knowledge spillovers (by defining the boundaries of the innovation), while the second increases spillovers (by providing information to competitors).

Almeida and Kogut (1995, 1) argue that "ideas, because they have no material content, should be the least spatially bounded of all economic activities." Accordingly, patents provide a paper trail for the flow of ideas from one innovator to another. Citations in a patent are used to delimit the scope of the property right conveyed by the patent. A citation of *X* by *Y* means that *Y* builds upon *X*; therefore the more *citations* within a firm's patent filing, the smaller will be the scope of the monopoly held by the patent holder. Therefore, the scope of that firm's invention will be reduced accordingly. A citation of *X* by *Y* and then of *Y* by *Z* provides a paper trail for the technology diffusion process.

The use of patent citations to examine technology spillovers was first suggested by Jaffe (1989) and Jaffe et al. (1993) who examined the location of university and large firm patents in the United States in 1975 and 1980. Acs, Audretsch, and Feldman (1994) looked at corporate patenting by U.S. states and found evidence of geographic concentration.

Almeida and Kogut (1995) expand on this work by focusing on the geographic spillovers from patenting in the semiconductor industry, examining the role played by migrating engineers with patents "under their belts," and the role of start-ups in technology spillovers. The authors use patent data on semiconductor inventions to address the question: Where do knowledge spillovers go? Do they go to nearby firms, firms in the same country, or do they "go global"?

The public finance literature on local public goods suggests that spillovers are geographically bounded (that is, the greater the distance from the original activity, the smaller the positive or negative externality [Eden and McMillan 1991]). If knowledge has the characteristics of a local public good (as in the publicness perspective we outlined previously), the general presumption would be that knowledge spills over to other agents in the same region, but not outside of that region.[9] This could happen for a number of reasons. In some cases, local environmental conditions or natural resource endowments will catalyze the development of various industries within a region (Porter 1992). In other instances, a single firm will spin off companies or otherwise provide a supply of employees to start-up companies in the same region (Moore 1986).

In either case, given a common historical background, most if not all firms within that region will embark upon a common technological trajectory. As these firms proliferate, related local industries or institutions (for example, universities) supplying these firms with production factors will also flourish, thereby reinforcing the movement along the localized technological trajectory (Acs, Audretsch, and Feldman 1994; Porter 1992).

Informal communication networks of managers/scientists may also arise as the geographic proximity of firms is relatively close, thus providing a cross-fertilization of ideas among the firms in a specific region (Rosenberg 1982; von Hippel 1988). Cross-fertilization may be further enhanced as managers/scientists move from firm to firm within a region (Almeida and Kogut 1995). Thus, as firms within a region possess similar endowments of physical and human capital, they will confront similar opportunities to learn, as well as develop similar proficiencies in the ability to "learn to learn" (Stiglitz 1987). Knowledge thus may become localized as firms within a region become proficient at absorbing knowledge diffused by cohorts.

Two other points with regard to the localization of knowledge are worth noting. First, Almeida and Kogut's (1995) results suggest that, even if certain knowledge is manifest in a relatively mobile form (for example, information contained in patent filings), complementary assets (for example, close proximity to university research labs and personnel) may not be as mobile, thus providing a further geographical restriction of knowledge diffusion. Second, and equally as important, is the notion that it may be less costly for firms to adopt technologies similar to those of its geographic neighbors. That is, if the firm is "near others technologically, it will receive benefits—in the form of improved technology and improved learning capabilities—which it would not receive if it decided to strike out on its own" (Stiglitz 1987, 132). In other words, localization may also be a *consequence* of the conscious effort on the part of a firm's managers to avail themselves of spillover opportunities.

Hence, when considering the MNE, a critical issue arises: Where should R&D be undertaken by the MNE? In terms of public policy, if the MNE conducts R&D outside of the home country, that country may lose most of the benefits of spillovers. Accordingly, such spillovers are a major reason why host countries want to attract MNEs: to access these potential externality gains (Cantwell 1991; *Economist* 1995; Harris 1991).[10]

So far in this essay, we have concentrated on the role of large multinationals in the production, diffusion, and spillover of technology. What do we know about the differences between large MNEs and small and medium-sized enterprises (SMEs)[11] in technology production? Are there differences between large and small firms in terms of their technology FSAs, technology transfer, and technology spillovers? We address these issues in the following section.

## Technology Production: Comparing SMEs and MNEs

An early comparison between large and small multinationals in terms of technology production was conducted by Giddy and Young (1982) in their work on nonconventional multinationals, that is, small MNEs and MNEs from poor or small countries. Giddy and Young found that nonconventional MNEs were less likely to be technology innovators and more likely to be fast followers or imitators. They were more likely to use joint ventures and licensing rather than wholly owned subsidiaries to enter host countries.

Oman (1984) reached similar conclusions in his work on new forms of international investment. These authors cited financial constraints and lack of cutting edge proprietary technology as reasons why nonconventional MNEs would be more likely to use alternative contractual forms for penetrating foreign markets.

More recent work shows that technological innovations emerge from both small and large firms. However, as Acs and Audretsch (1988) found, differences exist in the level of innovative activity between large and small firms as industry conditions change. Acs and Audretsch conclude that, similar to Winter's (1984) predictions, different economic and technological regimes exist across industries such that large firms account for most of the innovative activity in industries in which R&D is especially salient. At the same time, small firms account for a more significant proportion of innovative activity in industries in which small firms are few in number and in which skilled labor plays an important role. The authors later conclude that

> most industries exhibit decreasing returns to scale with respect to the output of innovations. However, this relationship is apparently sensitive to the technological environment. In low-technology industries, there is at least some evidence of increasing returns. (Acs and Audretsch 1991, 44)

This reinforces the notion that small and large firms are engaged in innovative activity to different degrees depending on the technological regime prevailing in a given industry.

Almeida and Kogut (1995) compare the innovative patenting activities of small and large firms in the semiconductor industry. The authors find that small firms tend to innovate in less crowded areas while larger firms dominate patenting in well-established areas. Part of the reason is that small firms tend to be start-ups, receiving funding to explore new fields. In addition, the research activities of small firms tend to be more geographically localized. The authors argue that this localization is because start-up firms are more closely tied into regional networks than are large firms, and that this is particularly true for semiconductor firms in Silicon Valley. This may imply a "dense national small firm network, with larger firms bridging nations" (Almeida and Kogut 1996, 21). The authors conclude that small firms innovate in order to benefit from their own research and their local innovatory network.

To the extent that organizations innovate, the opportunity arises for them to transfer that technology when and where appropriate. The simple transfer of technology (the acquisition element of the transfer process), however, is perhaps the least problematic aspect of technology transfer

(Tung 1994). With regard to the propensity to transfer technology, SMEs and MNEs both have demonstrated a need to transfer technologies to foreign affiliates and other partners.

Although both SMEs and MNEs primarily transfer technology from a parent firm to a foreign affiliate, that is, through the hierarchy, SMEs are in many cases more likely than MNEs to engage in joint ventures and other types of alliances (Gomes-Casseres 1995). Thus, it is more likely that SMEs will find it necessary to combine resources and efforts with alliance partners (in terms of licensing arrangements, equity ventures, nonequity ventures, and so on) in order to compete effectively (Teece 1992). This increases the likelihood that technology transfer by SMEs will cross organizational boundaries, increasing the complexity and risk of the transfer process.

Buckley (1995) has examined the technologies likely to be transferred by SMEs and has determined that three types are prevalent. Specifically, he has identified small-scale technologies, labor-intensive technologies, and specialized high-technology know-how as probable candidates for transfer by SMEs. While it seems likely that small-scale technologies and labor-intensive technologies would be internalized through parent-to-affiliate transfers, alliances may allow SMEs to take advantage of high-technology know-how. Through alliances, SMEs may seek to reduce the cost of know-how exploitation by allowing partners to perform noncore, yet capital-intensive, functions such as marketing, distribution, and production (Buckley 1995; Gomes-Casseres 1995).

As noted earlier, the transfer (or, conversely, acquisition) of technology is relatively straightforward. However, other aspects of the technology transfer process, such as assimilation, diffusion, and development, are more complex and less assured of success (Tung 1994). Wherever technology is transferred across borders, the likelihood of successful assimilation and utilization is at risk depending on the economic, sociocultural, and organizational differences between the transferring and receiving firms (Tung 1994). Furthermore, Kogut and Zander (1993), Teece (1977), and Cantwell (1991) among others, have shown that the transfer of knowledge across borders is increasing in difficulty as the tacitness of that knowledge increases. As such, certain technologies composed of a tacit component, such as organizational or managerial processes, may be exceedingly difficult to transfer across national borders.

The preceding factors can be applied to the discussion of differences between SMEs and MNEs. The effect of the complexity of technology assimilation and diffusion (not to mention development) on SMEs is not entirely obvious. First, it must be noted that SMEs, due to the relatively small size of their managerial population, are likely to lack the managerial resources of which MNEs can avail themselves. SMEs are less likely to use formalized methods of transfer such as written instructions, sending technical experts abroad, or providing formal training. The major method of technology transfer is on-the-job training and the supply of machinery and parts, according to Buckley (1995).

That being the case, SMEs are also less likely to be able to properly manage the technology transfer process when problems occur. These problems may be the result of differences in economic, sociocultural, or organizational environments in the case of technology transfer to alliance partners (Tung 1994). In the case of transfers to foreign affiliates, however, difficulties may still arise due to the tacit nature of the technology being transferred, especially where high-technology know-how is involved (as in the case of biotechnology and semiconductor firms), because of the managerial resources needed to manage the process successfully.

Furthermore, SMEs have significantly less financial resources available to them than do MNEs, thus making it more difficult for SMEs to devote specific personnel and/or funding to aiding the transfer process. As difficulties arise in assimilating and understanding the proper usage of transferred technologies, SMEs will have difficulty alleviating the concerns and addressing the assimilation deficiencies of foreign affiliates and/or alliance partners (Tung 1994).

In terms of the costs of technology transfer, as outlined in figure 1, our analysis suggests that SMEs may face higher transactions costs than large MNEs. Although SMEs, due to their relative size, benefit from reduced bureaucratic costs, they also have fewer resources to devote to search, negotiation, monitoring, and enforcement efforts. They may also be more subject to opportunistic behavior on the part of suppliers and buyers due to their smaller size and corresponding inability to retaliate. Being a small technology producer may imply lower costs of transmitting tacit knowledge within the enterprise as a whole; on the other hand, the costs of teaching and learning are more expensive for SMEs since they do not have "deep pockets."

Lastly, SMEs may be less likely to have a tight appropriability regime protecting their knowledge-based FSAs (for example, patents are an expensive and time-consuming process, as well as being geographically bounded) and therefore may face higher risks of dissipation and its attendant costs. As figure 2 suggests, SMEs may be less likely to own property rights to their technology assets, or to own complementary assets such as distribution networks.

In addition, Acs, Audretsch, and Feldman (1994) have suggested that large firm managers, frustrated by bureaucratization, may migrate to (or create) smaller firms in search of a less hierarchical organizational environment in which to utilize their skills. This may provide one mechanism by which small firms avail themselves of spillovers. Furthermore, spillovers to small firms seem to be largely dependent on university research. Thus, even if larger firms are successful in curtailing leakage of proprietary knowledge, localization may still proceed via university and small firm contacts.

Consideration of technology *consumption* suggests that technology spillover opportunities may be especially valuable to technology transferees that are small firms. Limited resources (for example, human and financial capital) may restrict the scope of small firms' research efforts in comparison to their larger counterparts. And, due to these restrictions, knowledge deficiencies may result. Spillovers may attenuate these effects as small firms acquire knowledge without the attendant acquisition costs. On the other hand, SMEs are less likely than MNEs to engage in FDI, alliances, or technology transfers in developing countries (Buckley 1995). This eliminates a key source of complexity in technology transfer processes (Tung 1994). Thus, it is not entirely clear that SMEs will have a more difficult time in successfully completing all phases of the technology transfer process.

In summary, small firms face additional financial constraints that raise the costs of technology production and transfer, relative to large multinationals. Thus, given the relative constraints facing SMEs regarding managerial and financial resources, these firms may face a higher failure rate in transfers of technology than will MNEs. Because of the probable relative gains to technology transfer accruing to SMEs, and the entrepreneurial nature of SMEs and their owners, the risk involved is simply a cost of doing business as a small, internationally oriented organization.

As methods to overcome the liabilities of their smallness, SMEs tend to use alliances and joint ventures rather than wholly owned subsidiaries as methods of entry into foreign markets, to focus on niche as opposed to commodity markets, and to use less formal methods of technology transfer. In the most successful cases, SMEs can be "mini-nationals" in global niche markets. As technology producers, the competitive advantage of mini-nationals comes not from size and deep pockets but from being lean, focused, and flexible; that is, from following the rules: "Do what you know how to do. Do it right. And do it everywhere" (*Business Week* 1993, 67).

## Conclusion

Multinational enterprises are the major global producers and disseminators of technology. The core competence of MNEs rests on their proprietary assets, the strength of which depends on the tightness of the appropriability regime protecting these assets. A tight appropriability regime can come from patents protecting public knowledge from dissipation through knowledge spillovers and opportunistic behavior, or from a high tacit component to the MNE's knowledge assets.

The MNE's mode of entry into foreign markets will depend partly on the relative knowledge transfer costs of using the external market versus the hierarchy. These costs include costs of making transactions, the risks of opportunism and dissipation of FSAs, and the costs of disseminating tacit knowledge. Technology spillovers tend to be localized because, even if the public component is high, technology has a tacit component that reduces the spillover range.

For small and medium-sized enterprises, the costs of technology production and transfer are high. As a result, SMEs tend to use less conventional methods: they rely more on joint ventures and alliances, they use less formal methods of technology transfer, and they focus on niche markets. The most successful SMEs, due to their competitive advantage in flexibility, can become mini-nationals. This suggests that technology production need not always be the sine qua non of large multinationals; small and medium-sized enterprises can also become active technology producers in the global economy.

## NOTES

An earlier draft of this essay was presented by Lorraine Eden at the "Small and Medium-Sized Enterprises and the Global Economy: Trends and Patterns in Foreign Direct Investment" seminar, CIBER, University of Maryland, Oct. 20, 1995. The authors would like to thank Zoltan Acs for providing helpful advice and background materials on SMEs, and two anonymous referees for their comments on the essay.

1. See, for example, chapter 6, "Transnational Corporations, Technology and Growth," in *World Investment Report 1992.*

2. We consider technology and knowledge to be the same in this essay. Following Dunning (1988, 287) we define technology as the "output of technological and organizational capacity, which determines the way (or ways) in which tangible and intangible resources may be physically converted into intermediate and finished goods and services."

3. *Jointness* means that once a good is produced the marginal cost of extending provision to an additional consumer is zero or near zero. That is, the use by one agent has no impact on the amount available for use by others. The opposite of jointness is rivalness; that is, if increasing the number of consumers from $N$ to $N + 1$ reduces my share from $1/N$ to $1/(N + 1)$ the good is rival; if my share remains $1/N$ as $N$ rises, the good is joint. Jointness fails, for example, if increasing the number of consumers creates congestion costs. Note that even if the marginal cost of provision is zero, the price will be nonzero since costs of production must be covered if the good is to be

produced at all. The key is that, once the good is produced, the marginal cost of adding an additional consumer is zero (Eden and McMillan 1991).

4. Nonexcludability means that the price system cannot be used to ration consumption of the good. Price exclusion may not be feasible for institutional reasons (such as a lack of assigned property rights) or for technological reasons (for example, national defense) or because consumer preferences cannot be ascertained due to preference revelation problems. Where exclusion is not possible, self-interested consumers are likely to free ride, leading to underprovision of the good or service (Eden and McMillan 1991).

5. Johnson (1970) even suggests that free riding (underpayment for technology transfers) might be acceptable, on equity grounds, for developing countries that have little chance of becoming home countries for MNEs.

6. This is the "fresh winds of competition" argument often used by Canadian economists as one of the arguments in favor of Canada-U.S. free trade (Lipsey, Schwanen, and Wonnacott 1995).

7. This latter effect is akin to the congestion effects of local public goods, where the addition of more consumers causes congestion that reduces the benefit to the existing agents (Eden and McMillan 1991).

8. For a thorough literature review on the theory and empirical work on technology spillovers, together with some new estimates, see Kokko 1992.

9. However, the reverse view is suggested by the theory of epistemic communities, as developed in the field of international political economy (Haas 1989). An epistemic community is a group of like-minded scholars that share the same beliefs and goals (for example, the "green" coalition of environmental activists, ecology experts, and university scientists); such communities often span several countries. Ideas may have greater mobility—spread more easily and quickly—within an international epistemic community than within a country.

10. For a more thorough discussion of the locality considerations surrounding R&D, see the work of Pearce (1989) and Casson (1991).

11. Note that the definition of a small and medium-sized enterprise must be made relative to the size of the market. A small firm selling only in a niche market may hold the largest share of that market and therefore be a "large" firm. Our definition of SMEs assumes that the firms are small relative to the size of the market.

## REFERENCES

Acs, Z. J., and D. B. Audretsch. 1988. "Innovation in Large and Small Firms: An Empirical Analysis." *American Economic Review* 78:678–90.

———. 1991. "R&D, Firm Size, and Innovations Activity." In Z. J. Acs and D. B. Audretsch, eds., *Innovation and Technological Change*, 39–60. Ann Arbor: University of Michigan Press.

Acs, Z., D. B. Audretsch, and M. Feldman. 1994. "R&D Spillovers and Innovative Activity." *Managerial and Decision Economics* 15:131–38.

Almeida, P., and B. Kogut. 1995. "The Geographic Localization of Ideas and the Mobility of Patent Holders." Paper presented at the "Small and Medium-Sized Enterprises and the Global Economy: Trends and Patterns in Foreign Direct Investment" seminar, CIBER, University of Maryland, Oct. 20.

Arthur, W. B. 1988. "Self-Reinforcing Mechanisms in Economics." In Philip W. Anderson, Kenneth J. Arrow, and David Pines, eds., *The Economy as an Evolving Complex System,* 9–31. Reading, MA: Addison-Wesley.

Buckley, P. J. 1995. "International Technology Transfer by Small and Medium Sized Enterprises." Paper presented at the "Small and Medium-Sized Enterprises and the Global Economy: Trends and Patterns in Foreign Direct Investment" seminar, CIBER, University of Maryland, Oct. 20.

Buckley, P. J., and M. Casson. 1976. *The Future of the Multinational Enterprise.* London: Macmillan.

*Business Week.* 1993. "Mini-nationals Are Making Maximum Impact." Sept. 6, 66–69.

Cantwell, J. 1989. *Technological Innovation and Multinational Corporations.* Oxford: Basil Blackwell.

———. 1991. "The Theory of Technological Competence and Its Application to International Production." In D. McFetridge, ed., *Foreign Investment, Technology and Economic Growth.* Industry Canada Research Series, vol. 1. Calgary: University of Calgary Press.

Casson, M. 1982. "Transactions Costs and the Theory of the Multinational Enterprise." In A. Rugman, ed., *New Theories of the Multinational Enterprise.* London: Croom Helm.

———. 1991. *Global Research Strategy and International Competitiveness.* Oxford: Basil Blackwell.

Caves, R. 1996. *Multinational Enterprises and Economic Analysis.* 2d ed. Cambridge: Cambridge University Press.

Dunning, J. 1988. *Multinationals, Technology and Competitiveness.* London: Allen and Unwin.

———. 1993. *Multinational Enterprises and the Global Political Economy.* Reading, MA: Addison-Wesley.

*The Economist.* 1995. "Of Strategies, Subsidies and Spillovers." March 18.

Eden, L. Forthcoming. *Taxing Multinationals: Transfer Pricing and Corporate Income Taxation in North America.* Toronto: University of Toronto Press.

Eden, L., and M. McMillan. 1991. "Local Public Goods: Shoup Revisited." In Lorraine Eden, ed., *Retrospectives on Public Finance.* Durham, NC: Duke University Press.

Giddy, I., and S. Young. 1982. "Conventional Theory and Unconventional Multinationals: Do New Forms of Multinational Enterprise Require New Theories?" In A. Rugman, ed., *New Theories of the Multinational Enterprise.* London and Canberra: Croom Helm.

Gomes-Casseres, B. 1995. "Alliance Strategies of Small Firms." Paper presented at the "Small and Medium-Sized Enterprises and the Global Economy: Trends and Patterns in Foreign Direct Investment" seminar, CIBER, University of Maryland, Oct. 20.

Haas, P. 1989. "Do Regimes Matter? Epistemic Communities and Mediterranean Pollution Control." *International Organization* 43 (3): 377–403.

Hamel, G. 1991. "Competition for Competence and Inter-partner Learning Within International Strategic Alliances." *Strategic Management Journal* 12:83–103.

Harris, R. 1991. "Strategic Trade Policy, Technology Spillovers and Foreign Investment." In D. McFetridge, ed., *Foreign Investment, Technology and Economic Growth.* Industry Canada Research Series vol. 1. Calgary: University of Calgary Press.

Hennart, J. F. 1991. "The Transaction Cost Theory of the Multinational Entreprise." In C. Pitelis and R. Sugden, eds., *The Nature of the Transnational Firm.* London: Routledge.

Hood, N., and S. Young. 1979. *European Development Strategies of U.S. Owned Companies in Scotland.* Edinburgh: HMSO.

Jaffe, A. 1989. "Real Effects of Academic Research." *American Economic Review* 89:957–70.

Jaffe, A., M. Trajtenberg, and R. Henderson. 1993. "Geographic Location of Knowledge Spillovers as Evidenced by Patent Citations." *Quarterly Journal of Economics* 108:577–99.

Johnson, H. 1970. "The Efficiency and Welfare Implications of the International Corporation." In C. Kindleberger, ed., *The International Corporation.* Cambridge: MIT Press.

Kogut, B., and U. Zander. 1992. "Knowledge of the Firm, Combinative Capabilities, and the Replication of Technology." *Organization Science* 3:383–97.

———. 1993. "Knowledge of the Firm and the Evolutionary Theory of the Multinational Corporation." *Journal of International Business Studies* 24:625–45.

———. 1995. "Knowledge, Market Failure and the Multinational Enterprise: A Reply." *Journal of International Business Studies* 26:417–26.

Kokko, A. 1992. *Foreign Direct Investment, Host Country Characteristics, and Spillovers.* Stockholm, Sweden: The Economic Research Institute, Stockholm School of Economics.

Levin, R. C., A. K. Klevorick, R. R. Nelson, and S. G. Winter. 1987. "Appropriating the Returns from Industrial Research and Development." *Brookings Papers on Economic Activity* 3:783–820.

Lipsey, R., D. Schwanen, and R. Wonnacott. 1995. *The NAFTA: What's In, What's Out, What's Next.* Toronto: C. D. Howe Institute.

McFetridge, D. 1995. "Knowledge, Market Failure and the Multinational Enterprise: A Comment." *Journal of International Business Studies* 26:409–15.

Moore, G. E. 1986. "Entrepreneurship and Innovation: The Electronic Industry." In R. Landau and N. Rosenberg, eds., *Positive Sum Strategy,* 424. Washington, DC: National Academy Press.

Nelson, R. R., and S. G. Winter. 1982. *An Evolutionary Theory of Economic Change.* Cambridge: Belknap Press.

Office of Technology Assessment (OTA). 1994. *Multinationals and the US Technology Base.* Washington, DC: U.S. Congress.

Oman, C. 1984. *New Forms of International Investment in Developing Countries.* Paris: Development Center, OECD.

Patel, P., and K. Pavitt. 1991. "Large Firms in the Production of the World's Technology: An Important Case of 'Non-Globalization.' " *Journal of International Business Studies* 22 (1): 1–21.

Pearce, R. D. 1989. *The Internationalization of Research and Development by Multinational Enterprises.* New York: St. Martin's Press.

Porter, M. E. 1992. *The Competitive Advantage of Nations.* New York: The Free Press.

Rosenberg, N. 1982. *Inside the Black Box: Technology and Economics.* Cambridge: Cambridge University Press.

Rugman, A. M. 1981. *Inside the Multinationals: The Economics of Internal Markets.* New York: Columbia University Press.

———. 1986. "New Theories of the Multinational Enterprise: An Assessment of Internalization Theory." *Bulletin of Economic Research* 38 (2): 101–18.

Schumpeter, J. A. 1934. *The Theory of Economic Development.* Cambridge, MA: Harvard University Press.

Stiglitz, J. E. 1987. "Learning to Learn, Localized Learning and Technological Progress." In P. Stoneman, ed., *Economic Policy and Technological Performance,* 125–53. Cambridge: Cambridge University Press.

Teece, D. J. 1977. "Technology Transfer by Multinational Firms: The Resource Cost of Transferring Technological Knowhow." *Economic Journal* 87:242–61.

———. 1987. "Profiting from Technological Innovation: Implications for Integration, Collaboration, Licensing and Public Policy." In David Teece, ed., *The Competitive Challenge.* Cambridge: Ballinger.

———. 1988. "Technological Change and the Nature of the Firm." In G. Dosi, C. Freeman, R. Nelson, G. Silverberg, and L. Soete, eds., *Technical Change and Economic Theory*, 256–81. London: Pinter.

———. 1992. "Foreign Investment and Technological Development in Silicon Valley." *California Management Review* 34 (2): 88–106.

Tung, R. L. 1994. "Human Resource Issues and Technology Transfer." *International Journal of Human Resource Management* 5:808–25.

United Nations Center on Transnational Corporations (UNCTC). 1992. *World Investment Report 1992: Transnational Corporations as Engines of Growth.* New York: United Nations.

von Hippel, E. 1988. *The Sources of Innovation.* New York: Oxford University Press.

Winter, S. 1984. "Schumpeterian Competition in Alternative Technological Regimes." *Journal of Economic Behavior and Organization* 5:287–320.

# PART 4

# Technology Transfer in the Global Economy

# International Technology Transfer by Small and Medium-Sized Enterprises

*Peter J. Buckley*

This essay attempts to summarize the key issues involved in the international transfer of technology by small and medium-sized enterprises (SMEs). It focuses on what is new in the area and relies for its empirical evidence largely on the UNCTAD report on small and medium-sized transnational corporations (UNCTAD 1993).

After a brief review of the role of SMEs in the world economy, section 3 of the essay examines theoretical approaches to the internationalization of SMEs. Section 4 attempts to reconcile internationalization approaches to globalization. Section 5 examines the technology transfer strategies of SMEs, and section 6 focuses on types of technology transfer and managerial strategies. Section 7 provides conclusions.

## Small and Medium-Sized Enterprises in the World Economy

Small and medium-sized enterprises (SMEs) (here the working definition of a company with less than 500 employees is used) play an important role in the world economy as employment generators, as innovators and as exporters. They are important job generators because they tend to be more labor-intensive than larger firms, and as well as internal growth of SMEs, much job creation is the result of small business start-ups. The extent of innovation by SMEs, as opposed to large firms, is controversial, and it is clear that their exporting potential is generally less than that of large firms. Nevertheless SMEs have a crucial role to play in developing and transferring certain types of technology, and where there is a satisfactory niche for small firms, they can play a critical role in technological advances.

In terms of their international role, it is clear that SMEs account for a relatively small proportion of world foreign direct investment (FDI), but this proportion is growing. Global figures for SME FDI as a proportion of the total are unavailable (UNCTAD 1993). Some information is available on a national basis, however. Unfortunately each major source country keeps the information on a different basis and uses a different definition of "small" (or SME). This makes aggregation impossible. Representative figures for the United States (tables 1 and 2) show some important regularities. However transnational corporations (TNCs) are measured, they represent a high proportion of outward investment in terms of numbers in each of these major source countries (28.3 percent of parent firms investing abroad in the United States [5.5 percent of all foreign affiliates] in 1988, 39.8 percent of equity investment in Japan in 1991, 66.3 percent of foreign investors in the

**Table 1. United States: Shares of Parent Firms and Foreign Affiliates of Small and Medium-Sized Transnational Corporations in Those of All Transnational Corporations, by Industry of Parent Firms, 1988 (in percentages)**

| Industry | Number of Parent Firms | Foreign Affiliates | | | |
|---|---|---|---|---|---|
| | | Number | Assets | Sales | Employment |
| Primary | 40.6 | 6.1 | 5.7 | 0.1[a] | 6.9 |
| Agriculture, forestry, and fishing | 66.7 | 15.6 | 4.5 | 3.2 | 10.3 |
| Mining and petroleum | 38.0 | 5.8 | 5.7 | 0.1[a] | 6.5 |
| Manufacturing | 19.8 | 3.3 | 0.8 | 0.8 | 1.1 |
| Food, beverages, and tobacco | 19.2 | 1.3 | 0.2 | 0.3 | 0.3 |
| Textile products and apparel | 23.5 | 8.9 | 3.9 | 3.1 | 6.5 |
| Lumber, wood, and paper products | 17.2 | 3.8 | 1.1 | 1.1 | 0.9 |
| Chemicals and allied products | 17.6 | 2.2 | 0.7 | 0.6 | 0.6 |
| Primary and fabricated metals | 24.8 | 6.4 | 1.7 | 2.3 | 2.1 |
| Machinery, except electrical | 25.0 | 5.7 | 1.2 | 1.2 | 1.8 |
| Electrical and electronic equipment | 21.3 | 4.7 | 2.6 | 3.4 | 2.6 |
| Transportation equipment | 8.0 | 0.5 | — | 0.1 | 0.2 |
| Other manufacturing | 17.1 | 3.0 | 0.8 | 1.0 | 1.1 |
| Services | 39.9 | 12.8 | 4.1 | 3.2[a] | 3.1[a] |
| Wholesale and retail trade | 44.7 | 30.4 | 11.3 | 4.3[a] | 4.5 |
| Finance (except banking), insurance, and real estate | 59.4 | 4.6 | 2.2 | 2.2 | 1.0 |
| Hotels and other lodging places | 20.0 | 21.2 | 23.0 | | |
| Construction | 27.6 | 7.0 | 8.7 | 3.0 | 0.6 |
| Transportation, communication, and public utilities | 13.6 | 5.4 | 0.6 | 0.7 | 0.7 |
| Other services | 23.2 | 7.6 | 4.1 | 3.6[a] | 4.6[a] |
| All industries | 28.3 | 5.5 | 2.7 | 3.4 | 1.9 |

*Source:* Based on special tabulation of U.S. TNCs by firm size by U.S. Department of Commerce at the request of UN Conference on Trade and Development, Programs on Transnational Corporations; UNCTAD 1993, 66.

[a]Excludes data that are suppressed to avoid disclosure; thus, the figures are underestimated.

United Kingdom in 1981, 74 percent of all transnational corporations in Sweden in 1987, and 60.2 percent of all Italian transnational corporations and 28.8 percent of foreign affiliates in 1987). However, when we look at SMEs' contribution to aggregates such as foreign assets, sales, or employment, the picture changes dramatically. For these same years, SMEs accounted for 2.7 percent of foreign assets, 3.4 percent of foreign sales, and 1.9 percent of foreign employment for the United States; 0.8 percent of the book value of foreign direct investment of the United Kingdom; 2 percent of employment in Swedish-owned foreign affiliates; and 7.4 percent of employment and 6.2 percent of turnover in Italian transnational companies.

The UNCTAD survey did show foreign direct investment by SMEs to be growing rapidly. Table 3 shows that they are rapidly becoming more international. We should also note that SMEs that do internationalize tend to be larger, more capital-rich, more productive and profitable, and to have

**Table 2. United States: Shares of Foreign Affiliates of Small and Medium-Sized Transnational Corporations in Those of All Transnational Corporations, by Host Country, 1988 (in percentages)**

| Country | Number of Affiliates | Assets of Affiliates | Sales of Affiliates | Employment of Affiliates |
|---|---|---|---|---|
| Developed countries | 5.7 | 2.0 | 2.5 | 1.7 |
| Canada | 9.1 | 2.1 | 1.9 | 1.9 |
| Europe | 5.3 | 1.2 | 1.8 | 1.6 |
| Japan | 4.8 | | | 1.6 |
| Others | 3.4 | | | 1.4 |
| | | | | |
| Developing economies | 4.7 | 4.9 | 8.0 | 2.6 |
| Africa | 5.2 | 2.7 | 4.4 | 2.9 |
| South and East Asia | 5.8 | 9.9 | 17.6 | 4.2 |
| Hong Kong | 8.0 | 5.1 | 5.1 | 9.7 |
| Philippines | 4.4 | | | 3.4 |
| Republic of Korea | 3.1 | | | |
| Singapore | 5.3 | | | 2.6 |
| Taiwan Province of China | 6.0 | 2.5 | 5.4 | 5.1 |
| Latin America | 3.8 | 3.1 | 1.8 | 1.7 |
| Argentina | 1.3 | 0.2 | 0.3 | 0.4 |
| Brazil | 3.5 | 0.6 | 0.8 | 0.8 |
| Colombia | 3.4 | 1.0 | 1.0 | 2.0 |
| Mexico | 2.8 | 2.2 | 1.7 | 1.4 |
| Venezuela | 3.0 | 1.5 | 1.7 | |
| Middle East | 8.4 | 6.1 | 11.7 | 7.1 |
| | | | | |
| All countries | 5.5 | 2.7 | 3.4 | 1.9 |

*Source:* Based on special tabulation of U.S. TNCs by firm size by U.S. Department of Commerce at the request of UN Conference on Trade and Development, Programs on Transnational Corporations; UNCTAD 1993, 67.

**Table 3. Distribution of Foreign-Direct-Investment Cases by Small and Medium-Sized Enterprises, by Period (in percentages)**

| Country/Industry | Number of Investments Surveyed | Distribution by Period: Before 1949 | 1950–59 | 1960–69 | 1970–79 | 1980–89 | 1990–92 |
|---|---|---|---|---|---|---|---|
| | | | | By Home Country | | | |
| Japan | 142 | — | 1 | 5 | 25 | 55 | 15 |
| United States | 24 | 8 | — | 4 | 42 | 37 | 8 |
| Europe | 57 | — | — | 7 | 23 | 51 | 19 |
| All countries | 22 | 1 | — | 5 | 27 | 52 | 15 |
| | | | | By Industry of Parent Firm | | | |
| Primary | 5 | — | — | 20 | — | 80 | — |
| Manufacturing | 156 | 1 | — | 6 | 29 | 49 | 15 |
| High-technology industries | 33 | 6 | — | 6 | 21 | 55 | 12 |
| Medium-technology industries | 71 | — | — | 4 | 37 | 44 | 15 |
| Low-technology industries | 52 | — | — | 10 | 23 | 52 | 15 |
| Services | 67 | — | 1 | 1 | 24 | 57 | 16 |
| All industries | 228 | 1 | — | 5 | 27 | 52 | 15 |
| | | | | By Host Country | | | |
| Developed countries | 129 | 2 | — | 5 | 27 | 51 | 15 |
| United States | 42 | — | — | 5 | 21 | 64 | 10 |
| Europe | 72 | 1 | — | 6 | 29 | 46 | 18 |
| Others | 15 | 7 | — | 7 | 33 | 40 | 13 |
| Developing countries | 99 | — | 1 | 5 | 26 | 53 | 15 |
| South and East Asia | 91 | — | 1 | 5 | 26 | 54 | 13 |
| Others | 8 | — | — | — | 25 | 38 | 38 |
| All countries | 228 | 1 | — | 5 | 27 | 52 | 15 |

*Source:* Based on the UN Survey; UNCTAD 1993, 54.

a higher export ratio than SMEs in general (table 4). This is unsurprising, but it does produce a curious statistical artifact—SMEs which internationalize rapidly cease to be SMEs (on any of the definitions used)!

SMEs show a strong preference for nonequity forms of technology transfer such as licensing (rather than FDI). SMEs from advanced countries also concentrate their investments more in other advanced countries rather than in less developed countries (LDCs). In fact, their investments are locationally clustered near to the source country to a larger degree than large multinational companies (MNCs). This may be the result of limited horizons, risk aversion, and the influence of "psychic distance" (Hallen and Wiedersheim-Paul 1979), which all bear heavily on SMEs. Internationally oriented SMEs also tend to be industrially concentrated, specializing particularly in locationally bound services and manufactured and capital goods (UNCTAD

**Table 4. Comparison of Some Features of Small and Medium-Sized Manufacturing, Transnational Corporations with Small and Medium-Sized Manufacturing Enterprises in General**

| Features | Small and Medium-Sized TNCs[a] | SMEs in General |
|---|---|---|
| Size | | |
| Average sales worldwide (millions of dollars) | 89 | 3.3[b] |
| Average number of employees in home country | 286 | 30[b] |
| Average number of employees worldwide | 515[c] | — |
| Average capital worldwide (millions of dollars) | 42 | 0.3[d] |
| Average value added worldwide (millions of dollars) | 28 | 1.3 |
| Labor-capital ratio (number of employees/capital in millions of dollars) | 13 | 58[d] |
| Labor productivity (value added in millions of dollars/number of employees) | 0.06 | 0.04[b] |
| Capital productivity (value added/capital in millions of dollars) | 0.5 | 1.8[d] |
| Export ratio (export/sales, percentage) | 22 | 15[e] |
| Profit ratio[f] (profit/sales, percentage) | 7.9 | 4.2[d] |

*Source:* Based on the UN Survey; UNCTAD 1993, tables 1.1 and 1.5; and Ministry of Finance, *Zaisei Kinyu Tokei Geppo (Monthly Report of Fiscal and Financial Statistics)*, no. 462 (Tokyo: Ministry of Finance Printing Bureau, October 1990).

[a]Based on 62 firms for average sales worldwide; 47 firms for the average number of employees in home country and worldwide; 57 firms for average capital worldwide; 39 firms for average value added worldwide; 55 firms for labor-capital ratio; 39 firms for labor productivity and for capital productivity; 56 firms for export ratio; and 47 firms for profit ratio.

[b]Based on the data of Australia, Austria, Canada, France, Germany, Ireland, Japan, New Zealand, Norway, and the United States in table 1.1.

[c]There are a few firms with more than 500 employees in home country. These firms, however, employed fewer than 500 employees at the end of the 1980s, the criterion year in the United Nations Survey. These firms' data are included.

[d]Only Japanese SMEs.

[e]Data of France, Italy, Netherlands, and Norway in table 1.5 are used.

[f]Defined here as income (sales minus costs) before taxes divided by sales.

1993). It is against this background that the international technology transfer activities of SMEs need to be set.

## Theoretical Approaches to Internationalization by SMEs

In a previous essay (Buckley 1989), I reviewed the analysis of the internationalization of SMEs under four generic headings: the economics of the firm's growth, internationalization and evolutionary approaches to growth, the gambler's earnings hypothesis, and the corporate decision making approach. There is no point in reviewing each of these in detail again; instead, this essay attempts to synthesize the key issues and update the arguments. Several key arguments can be abstracted from the literature.[1]

First, there is an important relationship between the firm and the market. There is a crucial relationship between the firm's size and overall market size. In one polar case, we can envisage a small firm attempting to grow (internationalize) in a "big-firm" industry, that is, an industry where optimal scale is large in relation to market size. This poses problems in terms of resource acquisition, notably capital and management skills. In the other extreme case, there are industries with few economies of scale where many small firms prosper. Industries requiring a wide range of specialist intermediate inputs, in particular, present a small firm in equilibrium with a small market. Thus we can make a distinction between absolute smallness and relative smallness. The role of small firms in filling a niche market has been noted as a key attribute of third world multinationals whose key competitive advantage is their skill as versatile users of flexible equipment (Wells 1983). There is a case to be made that the current downsizing and moves toward "lean production" and outsourcing mean greater opportunities for smaller firms to fill new supply niches. Table 5 shows the view that SMEs that have already internationalized have of the problems or opportunities given by small size. It was felt to be more of a constraint than an advantage in R&D, finance, and recruitment of skilled employees. However, small-scale was more often seen as an advantage than a constraint in economies (or diseconomies) of scale, overseas marketing and distribution, and information capacity. These factors give clues to the types of industries, contexts, and markets in which SMEs' internationalization is likely to be successful. Where

**Table 5. Shares of Small and Medium-Sized Transnational Corporations That Think That Firm Size Constitutes a Constraint or an Advantage for Foreign Direct Investment**

| Category Associated with Foreign Direct Investment | Constraint | Advantage | No Difference |
|---|---|---|---|
| Research and development | 27 | 19 | 44 |
| Finance | 35 | 19 | 40 |
| Recruitment of skilled employees | 26 | 22 | 45 |
| Economies/diseconomies of scale | 21 | 26 | 45 |
| Overseas marketing/distribution | 27 | 42 | 29 |
| Information capacity | 23 | 32 | 35 |

*Source:* Based on the UN Survey; UNCTAD 1993, 136.
*Note:* Figures based on 108 company responses.

local skills are needed, small scale is a positive advantage, and information processing is required (speedily), then SMEs are likely to feel more confident of success.

Second, there are several important constraints on the international activities of SMEs. Perhaps the most important of these are internal constraints. Two key issues here are shortages of capital and of managerial skill. In raising capital, a small firm faces a catch-22 problem—how to raise financing without disclosing its competitive advantages (in particular its proprietary technology). These institutional difficulties of capitalizing knowledge are compounded by the necessity to retain (family) control. The shortage of skilled management in SMEs is often a more serious problem. Small firms typically do not have specialist executives to manage their international operations, nor do they possess a hierarchy of managers through which complex decisions can be filtered. Decision making is likely to be personalized, involving ad hoc, short-term reckoning based on individual perception and prejudice. (This not unknown in large multinationals!) A shortage of management time leads to the firm taking shortcuts without a proper evaluation of alternatives. Information costs bear heavily on small firms, and attempts to avoid or reduce these costs, for instance by making no serious attempt to evaluate a potential agent or joint venture partner, can be disastrous. The horizons of small firms are limited by managerial constraints, and there is little "global scanning" of opportunities. Therefore, when an opportunity presents itself, it is often seized without proper evaluation. Given this problem, why does the firm not recruit management from outside the firm? One problem is the desire of family-owned companies to retain control inside the family circle; the other is the difficulty in obtaining specialist knowledge of how to evaluate outsiders. Lack of these crucial evaluation skills constrains recruitment and makes endemic the burden on management. Consequently small firms with inexperienced managers can behave in a naive fashion, particularly outside their normal cultural milieu. They can be politically naive because they lack public relations skills, lobbying power, and the sheer economic muscle of larger firms.

The role of risk and uncertainty is an important one in determining SME internationalization patterns. It is likely that the proportion of resources committed to a foreign direct investment will be greater than for a large, diversified multinational. Failure is thus more costly. This can interact with information costs in a negative way, in that costly information collection will not be undertaken. Thus shortcuts or spurning of opportunities can result. Alternatively, owner-managers often act on impulse and are often greater risk takers than more 'managerialist' entrepreneurs. The rather erratic financial behavior of SMEs may also be explained by these factors. The gambler's earnings hypothesis highlights an important empirical phenomenon—a small initial foreign investment eventually leading to a large payback of profit in the form of dividends. An explanation is given by analogy with ploughing and harvesting. A period of ploughing may be set by the firm (say five to seven years). In this time the foreign subsidiary is given a great deal of freedom of action. After that the foreign subsidiary either generates a stream of income for the next project (the next ploughing) or it is sold off to obtain a return on the capital. The short decision-making horizon arises because of the restricted capital and management capacity. Thus a target rate of return and/or payback period are discovered by trial and error.

Fourth, we need to pay attention to the dynamics of growth in the industry. Large multinational firms often have highly sector-specific expansion routes. This leaves niche markets or "interstices" for SMEs to exploit. These niches are often in "small firm industries" or exist as a fringe in "large firm industries." SMEs may thus be pulled into foreign markets by large firms requiring suppliers or pushed abroad by increasing competition in home markets. The flexibility of SMEs in adjusting to external conditions needs to be set against their vulnerability to radical change in technological, political, institutional, and competitive conditions. The role of SMEs will vary over the life cycle of an industry. In the early stages, numbers of small firms will vie for position. As the industry matures, economies of scale become prevalent and only a few will survive. In the decline phase, established competitors will face a threat from new entrepreneurial, innovating SMEs (Vernon 1979).

Table 6 shows the relationships between SMEs and multinational firms both from the point of view of the SMEs' growth and in relation to their foreign direct investment. The relationship, of course, varies according to the type of industry, even when such broad industry groupings as these are used.

## Internationalization, Globalization, and SMEs

The motivation for SMEs to make foreign direct investments is remarkably orthodox. The three key motives that we observe for multinational companies—market seeking, resource seeking, and efficiency (low cost) seeking investments are all present in the list of motivations for SMEs, as they are for multinationals (Buckley 1995). In terms of market-related motivations, seeking growth in local markets is mentioned by 50 percent of the firms, strengthening competitive capacity by 27.3 percent, access to third country markets by 24.4 percent, and information gathering by 20.6 percent. Low cost labor is

**Table 6. Shares of Small and Medium-Sized Transnational Corporations That Think Their Relationship with Large Firms is Important in Their Growth and Foreign Direct Investment, by Area of Relationship and Industry[a] (in percentages)**

| | Area of Relationship with Large Firms | | | | |
|---|---|---|---|---|---|
| Industry | Customers/ Suppliers | Information Concerning Technical Development | Financial Services | Advisory Services | Marketing/ Distribution |
| | | | Firm's growth | | |
| Manufacturing | 37 | 25 | 5 | 7 | 30 |
| High-technology industries | 67 | 40 | — | 7 | 40 |
| Medium-technology industries | 26 | 20 | 3 | 3 | 26 |
| Low-technology industries | 35 | 23 | 10 | 13 | 29 |
| Services | 39 | 17 | 6 | 11 | 22 |
| All industries | 37 | 21 | 6 | 9 | 26 |
| | | | Foreign direct investment | | |
| Manufacturing | 16 | 7 | 6 | 9 | 15 |
| High-technology industries | 33 | 13 | 7 | 13 | 27 |
| Medium-technology industries | 14 | 6 | 3 | 3 | 9 |
| Low-technology industries | 10 | 6 | 10 | 13 | 16 |
| Services | 8 | 14 | 3 | 6 | 11 |
| All industries | 13 | 9 | 5 | 7 | 13 |
| | | | Both firm's growth and foreign direct investment[b] | | |
| Manufacturing | 14 | 7 | 2 | 5 | 11 |
| High-technology industries | 33 | 13 | — | 7 | 27 |
| Medium-technology industries | 11 | 6 | — | — | 6 |
| Low-technology industries | 6 | 6 | 6 | 10 | 10 |
| Services | 8 | 11 | 3 | 6 | 8 |
| All industries | 11 | 8 | 2 | 5 | 10 |

*Source:* Based on the UN Survey, UNCTAD 1993, 81.
[a]Based on 123 small and medium-sized TNCs.
[b]Answer to this is also included in separate responses to firm's growth and FDI.

mentioned by 14.5 percent and securing raw materials by 11.2 percent. This leads to a discussion of the overall strategies of SMEs in reaching foreign markets. Table 7 shows the degree of internationalization of SMEs in the UN Survey. SMEs in services were the most highly internationalized in terms of their FDI presence, followed by medium-technology industries, while low-technology industries had the highest proportion of exports to total sales followed again by medium-technology industries. It is possible to contrast internationalization with globalization. *Internationalization* is the term normally used for the gradual, sequential incremental approach described in Scandinavian literature (Johanson and Wiedersheim-Paul 1975; Johanson and Vahlne 1977), and by the studies carried out at Bradford (Buckley,

**Table 7. The Degree of Internationalization of Small and Medium-Sized Transnational Corporations**

| Industry | Proportion of Exports to Total Sales | Proportion of FDI to Total Assets |
|---|---|---|
| Manufacturing | 22 | 5 |
| High-technology industries | 10 | 5 |
| Medium-technology industries | 19 | 11 |
| Low-technology industries | 28 | 3 |
| Services | 14 | 20 |
| All industries | 18 | 15 |
| Number of companies observed | 81 | 66 |

*Source:* Based on the UN Survey; UNCTAD 1993, 88.

Newbould, and Thurwell 1988; Buckley, Berkova, and Newbould 1983). In contrast, the globalization approach suggests that firms can reach foreign markets in a simultaneous fashion—by a big bang.

Casson (1994) has attempted to synthesize these approaches by examining internationalization as a corporate learning process. He posits a model where the cost of acquisition of information about a market generates a set-up cost of entry. The sequential approach to entry hinges on the exploitation of systematic similarities between markets. Because of such similarities, experience acquired in one foreign market is of potential relevance to another. If foreign markets were all totally different from one another, then nothing learned in one market would have any significance for another. However, if markets are very similar, then a globalization pattern—a single discrete simultaneous entry into all markets—becomes feasible.

In a sequential approach, decisions about entering the second market are deferred until the first has been entered because this provides an option value that strengthens the case of sequential entry when some markets are only marginally profitable. However, this model assumes that each market is investigated before the local marketing strategy is determined. This can be contrasted with purely experimental learning where the market is entered *without* systematic investigation and learning results from responding to mistakes. The decision to learn by experience, Casson suggests, depends "first and foremost on the confidence of the management, and on the costliness of mistakes, and only peripherally on the issue of sequential entry" (1994, 15). Thus there is a key trade-off between exploiting economies of scope in knowledge (maximized by a sequential strategy), and the gains from exploiting profitable market opportunities without delay (a simultaneous entry globalization strategy).

Casson's piece is also illuminating on the issue of uncertainty. He suggests that there are two varieties of uncertainty facing the internationalizing firm. First, there is uncertainty about the state of the market (how similar it is to the home market and other previously entered markets). Second is the cost of collecting information to overcome this problem. The cost of collection depends on the type of market, which is not known in advance. The cost of "mistaken entry" may well be below that of systematic investigation; thus, making mistakes may be a rational way of expansion!

Table 8 shows the nature of the relationship between the foreign affiliate of the SMEs in developing countries and the parent firm. SMEs parallel multinational firms except that they are more conservative in conglomerate diversification abroad.

## Technology Transfer Strategies of SMEs

The UNCTAD study of technology transfer (1993), found that SMEs, like MNEs, transferred technology internationally that was overwhelmingly from their parent firms. They are thus not unbiased conduits but are vehicles for the international projection of parent firm-driven technology (98 percent of

**Table 8. Production Relationship between Foreign Affiliates in Developing Countries and Their Parent Firms[a]**

| Kind of Production Relationship | Affiliates of Small and Medium-Sized TNCs in Developing Countries | Affiliates of Large TNCs in Developing Countries |
|---|---|---|
| **Horizontal Relationship** | | |
| Producing the same products as parent firm with the same technology | 66 | 64 |
| Producing the same products as parent firm with different or modified technology | 23 | 29 |
| **Vertical Relationship** | | |
| Turning raw materals into semi-manufactured products | 15 | 19 |
| Turning raw materials into final products | 28 | 23 |
| **No Relationship** | | |
| Producing completely different or unrelated products | 10 | 14 |
| Number of companies observed | 79 | 129 |

*Source:* Based on the UN Survey; UNCTAD 1993, 99.

[a]As some of the affiliates are engaged in different lines of production, there is more than one production relationship; therefore, total adds up to more than 100.

affiliates; UNCTAD 1993, 106). Table 9 shows that SMEs do carry out a considerable amount of in-house R&D and that this is largely conducted in the home country. The most common vehicle for international transfer is via a joint venture with a host country company. Because SMEs have a constraint on their in-house set of capabilities (Penrose 1959), joining with others enables international expansion to become profitable by adding to those preexisting capabilities. A narrower range of technology is transferred through SMEs than MNEs; particularly lacking are transfers of management technology and marketing technology. This may be partly due to the mode of transfer (joint ventures); it may also result from the lack of development of these technologies in SMEs in general.

The UNCTAD survey shows that the means of technology transfer in SMEs is much less formalized than in MNEs. This is related to their management style and the crucial constraints just referred to. The channel of written instructions is used much less in SMEs than MNEs, partly because of

**Table 9. Research-and-Development Activities by Small and Medium-Sized Transnational Corporations**

| Country/Industry | Proportion of Small and Medium-Sized TNCs: That Carry Out R&D | That Have a Specialized R&D Department | That Have R&D Facilities Abroad | Ratio of Total R&D Expenditures to Sales | Ratio of R&D Expenditures Abroad to Total R&D Expenditures |
|---|---|---|---|---|---|
| | | | By Home Country | | |
| Japan | 66 | 34 | 7 | 1.0 | 4.3 |
| United States | 69 | 56 | 31 | 2.0 | 4.1 |
| Europe | 76 | 52 | 36 | 2.3 | 6.1 |
| All countries | 70 | 43 | 17 | 1.5 | 5.0 |
| | | | By Industry | | |
| Manufacturing | 81 | 55 | 18 | 2.0 | 5.0 |
| High-technology industries | 86 | 64 | 7 | 2.4 | 8.7 |
| Medium-technology industries | 85 | 59 | 24 | 2.2 | 3.5 |
| Low-technology industries | 74 | 44 | 19 | 1.0 | 5.2 |
| Services | 43 | 20 | 10 | 0.3 | 7.5 |
| All industries | 70 | 43 | 17 | 1.5 | 5.0 |
| Number of companies observed | 109 | 109 | 109 | 56[a] | 46[b] |

*Source:* Based on the UN Survey; UNCTAD 1993, 96.

[a]Ten out of 56 small and medium-sized TNCs report zero R&D expenditures.

[b]Thirty-four out of 46 small and medium-sized TNCs report zero R&D expenditures.

lack of personnel to codify the technology and partly because many of the skills in SMEs are acquired through personal experience. Sending technical experts abroad to aid in technology transfer is much more difficult for SMEs (the high opportunity cost of technical personnel is crucial here), and written instructions are used much less frequently. There is also less expenditure on specialized technical training to aid in the transfer. Only 40 percent of foreign affiliates of SMEs had technical training other than on-the-job training, compared to 70 percent for large firms (UNCTAD 1993, 109).

Typically, therefore, on-the-job training plus the supply of machinery and parts that embody the technology is the crucial transfer mechanism in SMEs. Manuals and technical handbooks are used by a minority of SMEs, and even blueprints and drawings are only utilized in 51 percent of cases.

Efforts are made to adapt technology to host country conditions. Key factors affecting adaptation are scale differentials, different factor endowments, and gaps in technological capabilities between source and host countries. However, the UNCTAD survey found that a lower percentage of SMEs than MNEs made efforts to adapt their technology (77 percent vs. 86 percent). Several reasons can be adduced for this dissemination: (1) SMEs have a lower level of technological mastery, (2) the reliance of SMEs on the experience of skilled technicians (including owners) and the custom-order nature of technology in SMEs reduce the need to formalize adaptation efforts (that is, the tacit component of technology is higher in SMEs), (3) barriers to adaptation (for example, poor local supplies) are greater for SMEs than MNEs, (4) adaptation may divert very scarce resources away from activities at home, and (5) the technologies transferred by SMEs may be inherently more suitable to LDCs than those of large companies—thus there is a reduced need to modify SME technology.

## Types of Technology Transfer by SMEs

Three types of technology may be picked out as appropriate for international transfer by SMEs: small-scale technologies, labor-intensive technologies, and specialized high-technology know-how.

In the first case, we can refer back to our earlier discussion of the firm and the industry. SMEs may be operating in industries where efficient scale is reached at a small volume of output relative to the total demand for the product. Thus the industry can accommodate a large number of SMEs. Second, there are industries where efficient scale is reached only at a large volume of production but demand still remains unsatisfied. Perhaps this is due to discontinuities in technology. One or two large plants of efficient scale do not satisfy demand, but unsatisfied demand is insufficient to attract a new entrant. Thus a fringe of SMEs fill unsatisfied demand. Third, SMEs can operate alongside large firms where there are not huge cost penalties in operating below efficient scale. Here, SMEs may use a different production mode, specializing in made-to-order, custom-built, or small-batch production.

These three situations are very different. Technologies transferred in the first and third situations will be viable alternatives to MNE technology. In the second situation, the risk is that SMEs will possess an inferior or second-best technology that will be vulnerable not only to technological change but also to changes in the competitive structure of the industry. Over time, the rate of decline of costs with respect to scale will be critical to the viability of SME-transferred small-scale technology.

In the case of labor-intensive technologies, it is obvious that SMEs operate in the most labor-intensive sectors—notably services—and therefore they may be more suited to the international transfer of more labor-intensive technologies. Here a distinction must be made between *processes* that are labor-intensive and *collections of activities* (as in normal industry and firm accounting) that are labor-intensive. It has long been observed that labor-intensive stages of production are relocated in cheaper labor locations (Vernon 1966) but this is mainly the prerogative of large, well-organized multinational firms. The relatively internationally unsophisticated SMEs are not in a position to reconfigure their activities globally, and it is usually the whole of productive activities that are relocated.

Third, new technologies are transferred internationally by SMEs; examples include biotechnology and microelectronics. We should also be wary of assuming that new technology aligns perfectly with industry (or even strategic group) divisions. Much new technology is disguised within traditional industries. SMEs face a general problem of capitalizing in-house knowledge. They therefore need external funding to develop and spread their innovatory developments. Going to the market can be risky, so firm to firm deals are often chosen to extend their range. Equity (joint ventures) and nonequity (licensing deals, alliances) routes are often used as a means of leveraging technology in a way that appears less risky than normal market capitalization.

## Managerial Processes in Small Firms and Technology Transfer

Chen and Hambrick (1995) found (in a study of airlines) that the small firms tended to be more active than large ones in initiating competitive moves, but in contrast large firms seemed to be more responsive when attacked. This is consistent with the flexibility and rapidity in strategy often ascribed to small firms. With regard to action visibility, small firms were likely to be more low-key and even secretive. The authors characterize actions as follows: "it appears that small airlines tend to hold their fire, calculating well developed, visible responses; large airlines act quickly but in rather straightforward, unexciting ways" (474). Hence the title of the essay: "Speed, Stealth and Selective Attack: How Small Firms Differ from Large Firms in Competitive Behaviour."

This stereotype of small firms as fast-moving opportunities may not be generalizable across industries or across cultures. Steinman, Kumar, and Wasner (1981) found that German medium-sized firms in the United States followed a rather cautious, managerialist approach to internationalization. Briemann (1989) found that smaller British firms invested in search of new markets, whereas German firms were more concerned with securing existing market positions.

The multinational research project on the international transfer of technology by small and medium-sized enterprises (Buckley et al. 1995) found that industry, national host, and source country factors influenced the form and nature of technology transfer but that idiosyncratic management influences were strong in SMEs.

## Conclusion

All the evidence suggests that SMEs will not, in aggregate, be the major suppliers and transferors of technology in the world economy, but they can fill crucial niche roles. The success of these niche roles will be partly determined by the key relationship between firm size and industry size and by SMEs being able to ride the dynamic of the industry. A second important success factor is the skill of management in SMEs being able to spot and to take opportunities in situations where resources are scarce and information is expensive.

The mechanism of transfer of technology in SMEs seems remarkably orthodox. In general, technology developed by the parent is transferred via an international network that relies rather heavily on joint ventures, alliances, and licensing links rather than on foreign direct investment. The key international transfer mechanism is on-the-job training in the host country.

The key technologies transferred are efficient small-scale technology, specialized custom-built or small-batch production technologies, and "opportunistic transfer" of technologies that in the long run will be more suited to larger firms. Managerial processes must play to the strengths of SMEs, including their ability to be flexible and to make rapid strategic moves.

## NOTES

1. Key references for each approach are as follows.

Economics of the firm's growth
Penrose 1959
Buckley and Casson 1976

Internationalization and evolutionary approaches
Buckley, Newbould, and Thurwell 1988
Nelson and Winter 1982
Vernon 1979
Buckley and Casson 1981

Gambler's Earnings Hypothesis
Barlow and Wender 1955
Penrose 1956

Corporate decision-making approach
Aharani 1966

## REFERENCES

Aharani, Yair. 1966. *The Foreign Investment Decision Process.* Boston: Harvard University.

Barlow, E. R., and I. T. Wender. 1955. *Foreign Investment and Taxation.* Englewood Cliffs, NJ: Prentice-Hall.

Briemann, Norbert. 1989. "A Comparative Study of Foreign Investment Decisions by Small and Medium-Sized British and German Manufacturing Companies." Ph.D. diss., Manchester Business School.

Buckley, Peter J. 1989. "Foreign Investment by Small- and Medium-Sized Enterprises: The Theoretical Background." *Small Business Economics* 1:89–100. Reprinted in Buckley and Ghauri, eds., 1993.

———. 1995. *Foreign Direct Investment and Multinational Enterprises.* London: Macmillan.

Buckley, Peter J., Zdenka Berkova, and Gerald D. Newbould. 1993. *Direct Investment in the UK by Smaller UK Firms.* London: Macmillan.

Buckley, Peter J., Jaimie Campos, Hafiz Mirza, and Eduardo White, eds. 1995. *International Technology Transfer by Small and Medium Sized Enterprises.* London: Macmillan.

Buckley, Peter J., and Mark Casson. 1976. *The Future of the Multinational Enterprise.* London: Macmillan.

———. 1981. "The Optimal Timing of a Foreign Direct Investment." *Economic Journal* 91:75–87.

Buckley, Peter J., and Pervez N. Ghauri, eds. 1993. *The Internationalisation of the Firm.* London: Dryden Press.

Buckley, Peter J., Gerald D. Newbould, and Jane Thurwell. 1988. *Foreign Direct Investment by Smaller UK Firms.* London: Macmillan. (Published in 1978 as *Going International—The Experience of Smaller Companies Overseas.* London: Associated Business Press.)

Casson, Mark. 1994. "Internationalisation as a Learning Process: A Model of Corporate Growth and Geographical Diversification." In V. N. Balasubramanyam and David Sapsford, eds., *The Economies of International Investment,* 238–52. Aldershot: Edward Elgar.

Chen, Ming-Jer, and Donald C. Hambrick. 1995. "Speed, Stealth and Selective Attack: How Small Firms Differ from Large Firms in Competitive Behaviour." *Academy of Management Journal* 38:453–82.

Hallen, Lars, and Finn Wiedersheim-Paul. 1979. "Psychic Distance and Buyer-Seller Interaction." *Organisation, Marknad och Samhalle* 16:308–24. Reprinted in Buckley and Ghauri, eds., 1993.

Johanson, Jan, and Jan-Erik Vahlne. 1977. "The Internationalisation Process of the Firm—A Model of Knowledge Development and Increasing Foreign Market Commitments." *Journal of International Business Studies* 8:23–32. Reprinted in Buckley and Ghauri, eds., 1993.

Johanson, Jan, and Finn Wiedersheim-Paul. 1975. "The Internationalisation of the Firm—Four Swedish Case Studies." *Journal of Management Studies* 12:305–22. Reprinted in Buckley and Ghauri, eds., 1993.

Nelson, R., and S. Winter. 1982. *An Evolutionary Theory of Economic Change.* Cambridge, MA: Harvard University Press.

Penrose, Edith T. 1956. "Foreign Investment and the Growth of the Firm." *Economic Journal* 66:230–35.

———. 1959. *The Theory of the Growth of the Firm.* Oxford: Blackwell.

Steinmann, H., B. Kumar, and A. Wasner. 1981. "Some Aspects of Managing U.S. Subsidiaries of German Medium-Sized Enterprises." *Management International Review* 21:27–37.

UNCTAD, Programme on Transnationals. 1993. *Small and Medium Sized Transnational Corporations: Role, Impact and Policy Implications.* New York: United Nations.

Vernon, Raymond. 1979. "The Product Cycle Hypothesis in a New International Environment." *Oxford Bulletin of Economics and Statistics* 41, no. 4:255–67.

Wells, Louis T. 1983. *Third World Multinationals: The Rise of Foreign Investment from Developing Countries.* Cambridge, MA: MIT Press.

# Conclusion

## Small and Medium-Sized Enterprises in the Global Economy

*Zoltan J. Acs and Bernard Yeung*

### Introduction

The essays in this book address the role of small and medium-sized enterprises in the global economy. While small and large firms are indeed different, to understand the role of small and medium-sized firms in globalization one may find it advantageous to make globalization the focus of the analysis. We advance a fundamental theme along this line: Globalization is the internationalization of Schumpeterian evolution (Schumpeter 1934), and small and large firms are co-dependent agents conducting the evolution.

The essay by Acs, Morck, Shaver, and Yeung explicitly proposes this theme. In addition, the essay by Dunning points out that in a globalized world, firm boundaries are reconfigured. The two pieces together imply that the distinction between large and small firms is analytically blurred because small and large firms are connected as a group in the internationalization of their individual skills and capabilities and of the synergistic capabilities they jointly create. The essays by Acs et al. and by Almeida and Kogut together imply that large and small firms are complementary in the discovery of capabilities. And the essay by Gomes-Casseres explicitly brings the co-dependence of large and small firms in leveraging their capabilities to the forefront. The purpose of this conclusion, therefore, is to explain this fundamental theme and as a consequence to connect research on small and medium-sized firms with mainstream economic thought.

### Globalization Is Internationalization of a Schumpeterian Evolution

To explain the theme, we need first to establish our interpretation of globalization. Three things stand out at the end of the twentieth century: the explosive growth in technology to connect people and locations, the creation of a freer environment for international trade and investment, and massive economic restructuring and liberalization. These events are the basis for globalization of business activities. Technological progress brings nations closer, and economic liberalization opens up economic opportunities. Profit-seeking firms and investors identify these new cross-border economic opportunities and act on them. The obvious consequences are huge cross-border flows of knowledge as well as goods and services. Cross-border intrafirm activities are now the norm rather than the exception.

We see globalization as a dynamic Schumpeterian evolutionary process (Schumpeter 1934) on a global scale. Imagine that the world is segmented by formidable natural and artificial barriers hindering information flow, trade and investment. The world changes; segmented localities are now physically connected by improved means of communication and transportation, and artificial barriers to information flow, trade, and investment have broken down. The old equilibrium, which is composed of autarky equilibrium in each segment, is not sustainable. The new environment has profitable trade and real investment opportunities that were previously unavailable because of natural (for example, high transportation costs) and artificial barriers (for example, trade and investment barriers). As firms and individuals actualize these opportunities, there will be international reallocation of production and factor inputs, changes in output and factor prices, and general changes in income and consumption patterns. The world undergoes structural adjustment.

The shift from the old equilibrium to the new equilibrium relies on the discovery and the appropriation of profit opportunities, which Kirzner (1997) refers to as entrepreneurial discovery. An integral component of globalization is therefore international expansion of firm operations, which is often typified by foreign direct investment. The following model is applicable not just to foreign direct investment; it applies to other forms of international expansion. For convenience, we start with a theoretically and empirically well received foreign direct investment theory, which is "internalization." In our opinion, the theory implies that international expansion of firm operations is a creative destruction process.

The internalization theory starts with the assumption that indigenous firms usually have the advantage over outsiders. The reason is that indigenous firms know more about the local environment and already have established relationships with vertically related business, ranging from intermediate good suppliers to local government to local consumers. Foreign entrants need to possess unique superior capabilities to overcome indigenous firms' home court advantage. These are information-based capabilities in technology, production, marketing, and management, which are often referred to as intangibles. Because they are information-based, intangible assets behave like public goods—they have intrinsic economies of scale and scope. Firms can leverage the value of their intangible assets by expanding their scale and scope of application. Due to well-known transactions difficulties in arm's-length trade of information-based assets, firms often have to retain direct control in expanding the application of their intangible assets. In other words, firms internalize the markets for their intangible assets. When firms expand the application of their intangibles internationally by retaining direct control of them, they become multinational firms. Empirical tests of the internalization theory in an international setting are reported in Morck and Yeung 1991 and 1992 and in a general setting in Morck and Yeung 1997.

Internalization implies that multinational firms manage to capture the overseas profit opportunities their intangibles create. The overseas profit opportunities exist because their intangibles allow them, as foreign entrants, to overcome local indigenous firms' home court advantage and thus to capture local indigenous firms' markets. In other words, firms are able to internationalize because of the superior competitive advantage of their intangibles. Recall that intangibles are information-based capabilities in marketing, production, and management. To the extent that local indigenous firms do not possess these intangibles, they are innovations from the perspective of local indigenous firms. *Seen in this light, a firm's cross-border expansion is an internationalized Schumpeterian evolution; and it is an indispensable component of globalization.*

## Small and Large Firms Are Globalization Partners

The essays in this volume suggest that internationalizing the Schumpeterian evolution is not a job for large or small firms in isolation. Rather, large and small firms are co-agents in the process.

Reynolds's essay raises the question whether the creation of a larger market favors larger firms. For example, did the creation of EU-1992 hurt the vitality of smaller firms in Europe? On the contrary, smaller firms' share of sales, value-added, and employment actually went up. In general, smaller firms in the 1990s increased their share in exports and in outward foreign direct investment in the OECD countries and in many Asian countries. Based on his literature survey, Reynolds concludes that new and small firms are major participants in international trade and are an independent source of economic growth. The implication is that globalization may actually be positively related to the vitality of smaller firms.

Dunning's article discusses in the context of globalization the changing boundaries of firms, markets, and nations. Dunning argues that the traditional firm boundaries are defined by ownership-conferred decision rights.

Globalization, however, has changed the nature of firm activities substantially. Technology allows firms to coordinate and cooperate globally. Due to reduction in trade and investment barriers, firms search globally for more efficient ways to serve customers and thus make more profits.

The result is internationalized competition. Firms have to go anywhere a component of the value chain is most efficiently supplied and to conduct a monstrous coordination job. Failing to do so will mean being outcompeted by those that have succeeded. Consequently, firms search for suitable resources, assets, and capabilities, and then match and coordinate them in generating goods and services for consumers. Firm focus is no longer purely on production; it becomes the coordination of "value-chain" activities ranging from design and R&D to sourcing to production and to marketing. In this new competitive landscape, firm boundaries are replaced by competing team boundaries. The assignment of multinational firms is now to seek and coordinate capabilities and to derive profits from its coordination capability.

## Multinationals Are Facilitators of Global Reach of Capabilities

This view is certainly in concordance with the perception that globalization calls for internationalization of the Schumpeterian evolution. Large multinational firms can now be thought of as global coordinators of capabilities possessed by groups of firm-units, some of which are small firms. They leverage these capabilities internationally and are essentially organizers of international Schumpeterian evolution.

The article by Acs et al. in this volume explicitly suggests that smaller and larger firms could have a synergistics relationship in the globalization effort. If the leader of the process of internationalizing Schumpeterian evolution (for example, a multinational firm) sees value in a small firm's capability, the small firm will be a component of the coordinated globalization effort. The small firm's contribution will be globalized indirectly in the form of acquisition, or arm's-length transaction, or hybrid dependence. From the small firm's perspective, it benefits from having an access to the multinational firm's global market reach. The consequence is not only that smaller firms' contribution is globalized, but their reward is increased because of the larger scope of applications of their contribution.

Acs et al. recognize that smaller firms can conduct international expansion on their own. They compare the two modes of international expansion: direct versus intermediated by a multinational firm. They argue that when a small firm conducts direct expansion it has to pay for the internationalization costs, which include market entry costs and property rights protection costs. In the intermediated mode, the small firm saves the internationalization costs but has to absorb some deadweight transactions costs and rent extraction by the intermediator. They argue that when competition among qualified intermediators bids away rent extraction, the private choice between the two modes of international expansion is socially efficient in the sense that the small firm's contribution is maximized.

Gomes-Casseres supports the suggestion in Acs et al. that small firms form partnerships with larger firms to globalize their market reach. Gomes-Casseres reports explicit examples that smaller firms form alliances with large firms to increase their capability to exploit their niche on a grander scale.

## Smaller and Large Firms Are Complementary Innovators

The basis of Schumpeterian evolution is the discovery of innovations. The essay by Acs et al. suggests that smaller firms are more likely to make radical innovations than larger firms and therefore are key contributors in the Schumpeterian evolution. The argument is worth repeating. The introduction and the article by Acs et al. point out that innovations arise only when property rights are properly aligned. Acs et al. argue that property rights may be less properly aligned in larger corporations than in smaller companies and among individual innovators. An innovator in a large company only has very limited property rights protection. The results of the innovation generally belong to the corporation, not the employee who invented it. This creates the tendency to free ride on others' innovative efforts in a large company. Some may argue that the agency problem can be alleviated by incentive contracts. However, incentive contracts within corporations have to depend on ex post innovative results. This creates the tendency for established innovators to entrench and stifle the emergence of radical innovations that undermine the value of old innovations. All these concerns reduce creativity within a large company. In contrast to innovative employees in large corporations, independent innovators can hold clear property rights, can have every incentive to undertake radical innovation, and can be largely free of red tape.

## Thus, Smaller Firms Are Better at Creating Radical Innovations

The essay by Almeida and Kogut argues further that small firms' approach to innovating may be different from large firms. They examine the innovation in the semiconductor industry regarding firms' exploration of technological diversity and their integration within local knowledge networks. Their comparison of the innovative activity of start-up firms and larger firms possibly suggests that small firms explore new and less crowded technological areas and are tied into regional knowledge networks to a greater extent than large firms. Their results, like the theoretical deduction in Acs et al., suggest that small firms are more likely to be explorers of new technological spaces.

Note that the articles by Acs et al. and Almeida and Kogut together suggest that small and large firms complement each other in generating technological innovations. Almeida and Kogut's results imply that small and large firms will together undertake a more comprehensive search of the technological opportunity set. The Acs et al. article suggests that small and large firms play complementary roles: small firms form radical innovations while large firms pursue the deepening of existing innovations.

## Small Firms with Niche Technological Innovations Internationalize Alone

There is no presumption that small firms do not initiate a Schumpeterian evolution process on their own. Small firms would want to internationalize their innovations on their own if the cost of doing so (mainly entry costs) were less than the cost of internationalizing via the intermediation of large firms (mainly transactions costs and rent extraction by the intermediating large firms). The essay by Kohn reports that smaller firms do internationalize on their own. These are small firms possessing R&D-related capabilities and often reside in less mature industries than other smaller firms. (On the other hand, larger firms that conduct foreign direct investment often reside in more mature industries than other larger firms.) One explanation for these smaller firms' tendency to conduct direct internationalization is that hierarchical control of their property rights is important for them to claim the first mover advantage of their innovations. In terms of the argument in Acs et al. (this volume), smaller firms equipped with production-related intangibles find that expanding the international application of these skills via intermediation by larger firms leads to high transactions and rent extraction costs and thus is inferior to direct international expansion.

In summary, our reading of the main message in the essays in this book is that small and large firms are co-agents in the internationalization of Schumpeterian evolution. Their respective searches for innovations together form a more comprehensive scan of possibilities, and there is often a symbiotic relationship in their effort to internationalize. The unit of analysis is not firm size. Rather, the fruitful avenue of thinking is what globalization is and how different size firms play different roles.

## Policy Perspectives

### The Speed of Internationalized Creative Destruction

The theme calls to our attention an often overlooked angle in public discussion on policies toward small and medium-sized firms in the era of globalization. Participants in the discussion often focus on the low level of international activities by small and medium-sized firms. Public discussion then turns to the causes of the observation and to policy remedies to raise small and medium-sized firms' international expansion. In light of the contribution of the essays in this book, we suggest that considering the extent of international expansion by small and medium-sized firms does not offer a complete view. Also, the focus should not be on international expansion per se, but on the essential economic meaning of international expansion. The fundamental policy question suggested by the previous essays in this volume is whether there is adequate or excessive international creative destruction.

The message in Acs et al. is worth repeating. They raise the question, Is more innovation always better? An increased rate of innovation is good in that it reduces production costs and/or increases consumer choice. These societal gains stem from the "creative" side of creative destruction. More rapid innovation may be bad insofar as it makes existing physical and human capital obsolete. In doing this it can disrupt careers and communities. These societal costs stem from the "destructive" side of creative destruction.

No well-accepted theory of a socially optimal rate of creative destruction currently exists. Many commentators are writing about the increased pace of innovation in the midst of globalization. The essays in this book certainly add credence to the view. Absent a framework to evaluate the optimal rate of creative destruction, judgments on the impact of increased rate of Schumpeterian evolution remain subjective.

### Policy Needs in the Internationalization of Small and Medium-Sized Firms' Innovations

A less ambitious question is whether there is market failure in the internationalization of small and medium-sized enterprises' innovations. The essays in this book suggest some avenues for investigation. There are two ways to internationalize small and medium-sized firms' innovations: direct international expansion by the smaller firm or intermediation through a larger firm. In the former, the return to the smaller firm is the revenue the smaller firm can collect minus entry costs. In the latter, the return to the smaller firm is the return the larger firm can collect minus the larger firm's entry costs and transaction costs, the rent it manages to extract from the smaller firm, and the smaller firm's own share of transaction costs. In the absence of rent extraction by the intermediator, the comparison of the two returns is identical to comparing the savings in entry costs in the direct international mode to the transaction costs due to intermediated international expansion. The outcome is socially efficient: choose the intermediated international expansion mode when the additional transaction costs are less than the savings in entry costs.

Thus, for the purposes of achieving efficient international expansion, it is necessary to suppress rent extraction by intermediators of small and medium-sized firms' innovation. A first pass policy suggestion is to assure competition among larger firms that are capable of serving as an intermediator of smaller firms' innovations. A conventional wisdom is that reducing direct entry of large foreign multinational firms protects domestic small and medium-sized firms and may then allow them to grow. The theme we identify in this book suggests the opposite: encouraging entry of foreign multinational firms may actually help to internationalize small and medium-sized firms' innovations and is beneficial to them.

Second, the preceding consideration suggests that public policies should aim to reduce transaction costs. Transaction costs stem from difficulties in writing complete contracts to safeguard property rights. Here, an increase in judicial efficiency and effectiveness that facilitates contractual agreements and raises contractual credibility is the remedy. Judicial efficiency and effectiveness have been emphasized in the law and economics and transactions costs literature (Masten 1998). Recently, its contribution to market economies is also identified in the financial economics literature (La Porta et al. forthcoming; Morck, Yeung, and Yu 1998).

Third, to the extent that both direct and intermediated international expansion have to overcome entry barriers and more internationalized Schumpeterian evolution is globally optimal, international efforts to reduce policy-induced entry barriers improves efficiency.

The policy needs identified from the theme (that globalization entails internationalizing Schumpeterian evolution) coincide with the liberalization trends in the World Trade Organization. The Uruguay Round of GATT includes the liberalization of restrictions on foreign direct investment and improvement on intellectual property rights protection. With respect to liberalization of foreign direct investment, the Uruguay Round Agreement has established new rules prohibiting local content requirements and various trade and foreign exchange balancing requirements. With respect to intellectual property rights, the agreement has established minimum standards for protection and enforcement. In contrast, prior standards simply called for governments to provide the same protection to foreign intellectual property as they afford to domestic intellectual property. These liberalization measures reduce artificial entry barriers and also reduce transaction costs.

## Future Research Questions

The preceding section identified important areas of future research. First, does globalization increase the rate of "creative destruction"? Also, is that welfare enhancing? To the best of our knowledge, direct empirical examination of the first question has not been attempted. However, in the economic growth literature, there is no absence of evidence that openness increases a country's growth rate. Is the positive relationship due to a higher creative destruction rate, or is it just that openness eliminates deadweight losses? If the former is of considerable economic significance and faster growth is always welfare enhancing, we have a case that even though we do not know what the optimal rate of creative destruction is, the current world benefits from a faster rate of creative destruction.

Additionally, the preceding section identified three areas of research that might improve our understanding of the process of Schumpeterian evolution. They are reducing barriers to entry (both domestic and global), reducing transaction costs in the bilateral exchange of nonstandardized goods between firms, and suppressing rent extraction by intermediators. A careful look at these areas suggests that while there is a rich literature on entry barriers and transaction costs, our understanding of rent extraction is much less perfect.

Intuitively, one would think that competition mitigates rent extraction. Yet, careful readers will quickly recognize that the problem is not so easily resolved. First, internationalizing innovations involves nonstandardized skills. The assumption that there are numerous potential suppliers of the skills is often not justified.

Second, even if there is no rent extraction at the outset, a large firm internationalizing a small firm's innovation can extract rent over time once specific assets and commitments are made. The belief that competition mitigates such rent extraction (time inconsistent behavior) often relies on the assumption that the rent-extractor faces high reputation costs in the future.

Reputation costs mitigate rent extraction, as long as the number of potential suppliers of internationalization skills is not trivial. However, in most of these cases, evaluating the contributions of innovation itself and of the skills for internationalizing it is highly complicated, thwarted by the inherent double moral hazard problem in the process and the uniqueness of each innovation. The internationalization of an innovation takes the joint effort of the innovation supplier and the internationalization agent, both of which have agency incentives and face information asymmetry. As such, the identification of cheating and rent-extraction behavior is likely very difficult, making the reputation cost argument hazardous to apply. Serious attempts to understand these problems are warranted.

## REFERENCES

Kirzner, Israel M. 1997."Enterpreneurial Discovery and the Competitive Market Process: An Austrian Approach." *Journal of Economics Literature* 35 (1): 60–85.

La Porta, Rafael, Florencio Lopez de-Silanes, Andrei Shleifer, and Robert W. Vishny. Forthcoming. "Law and Finance." *Journal of Political Economy.*

———. 1997. "Legal Determinants of External Finance." *Journal of Finance* 52:1131–50.

Masten, Scott. 1998. "Contractual Choice." In *Encyclopedia of Law and Economics,* ed. B. Boukaert and G. De Geest. Cheltham, UK: Edward Elgar Publishing.

Morck, Randall, and Bernard Yeung. 1991. "Why Investors Value Multinationality." *Journal of Business* 64 (2): 165–87.

———. 1992. "Internalization: An Event Study Test." *Journal of International Economics* 33:41–56.

———. 1995. "The Corporate Governance of Multinationals." In *Corporate Decision-Making in Canada,* ed. Ronald Daniels and Randall Morck, Industry Canada Research Series. Alberta, Canada: University of Calgary Press.

———. 1997. "Why Investors Sometimes Value Size and Diversification: The Internalization Theory of Synergy." Mitsui Life Financial Research Center Working Paper 97–9, School of Business Administration, University of Michigan.

Morck, Randall, Bernard Yeung, and Wayne Yu. 1998. "The Information Content of Stock Markets: Why Do Emerging Markets Have So Little Firm-Specific Risk?" The Davidson Institute Working Paper 44a (Aug.), University of Michigan.

Schumpeter, Joseph A. 1934. *The Theory of Economic Development.* Cambridge, MA: Harvard University Press.

———. 1950. *Capitalism, Socialism and Democracy.* 3d ed. New York: Harper.

# Contributors

Zoltan J. Acs, Merrick School of Business, University of Baltimore, Baltimore, MD

Paul Almeida, School of Business, Georgetown University, Washington, DC

Peter J. Buckley, Center for International Business, University of Leeds, Leeds, United Kingdom

John H. Dunning, Graduate School of Management at Rutgers University, Newark, NJ

Lorraine Eden, Department of Management, Texas A&M University, College Station, TX

Benjamin Gomes-Casseres, Graduate School of International Economics and Finance, Brandeis University, Waltham, MA

Bruce Kogut, Wharton School, University of Pennsylvania, Philadephia, PA

Tomás O. Kohn, School of Management, Boston University, Boston, MA

Edward Levitas, Department of Management, Texas A&M University, College Station, TX

Richard J. Martinez, Department of Management, Texas A&M University, College Station, TX

Randall Morck, Faculty of Business, University of Alberta, Alberta, Canada

Paul D. Reynolds, Paul T. Babson Professor in Entrepreneurial Studies, Babson College, Babson, MA

J. Myles Shaver, Stern School of Business, New York University, New York, NY

Bernard Yeung, School of Business Administration, University of Michigan, Ann Arbor, MI

# Index